The Practice of Healing Prayer

A How-To Guide for Catholics

D1227512

Other Books by Francis MacNutt

Can Homosexuality Be Healed?

Deliverance from Evil Spirits

Healing, 25th Anniversary Edition

Overcome by the Spirit

Praying for Your Unborn Child (co-authored with Judith MacNutt)

The Healing Reawakening

The Prayer That Heals

The Power to Heal

The Practice of
Healing Prayer

A How-To Guide for Catholics

ask in Jesus name
P. 21.

Francis MacNutt, PhD

Cast out Demons. P. 23

the WORD
among us®
press

The Word Among Us Press
7115 Guilford Drive, Suite 100
Frederick, Maryland 21704
www.wau.org

19 18 17 16 15   6 7 8 9 10

ISBN: 978-1-59325-140-6
eISBN: 978-1-59325-402-5

Cover design by Faceout Studio

Made and printed in the United States of America

Library of Congress Cataloging-in-Publication Data

MacNutt, Francis.
  The practice of healing prayer : a how-to guide for Catholics / Francis MacNutt.
      p. cm.
  Includes bibliographical references (p.   ).
  ISBN 978-1-59325-140-6
  1. Spiritual healing--Catholic Church. 2. Prayer--Catholic Church. I. Title.
  BT732.5.M345 2010
  234'.131--dc22
                              2010020371

TABLE OF CONTENTS

To Judith, my beloved wife and partner
in the healing ministry, devoted mother of Rachel and
David, and cofounder of Christian Healing Ministries,
Jacksonville, Florida.

A Special Word
of Introduction

As I begin writing this book, I am excited and filled with enthusiasm because it gives me a chance to share with you a discovery that has transformed my life—and that I hope will change yours too. What I most want to share with you is that God still heals sick people when we pray with them—physically, emotionally, and spiritually. And this is not rare; it is common for people to be healed when we pray.

All of us know that when we come down with an illness, we should visit a physician as soon as possible to get the medical help we need. But not everyone knows that we can also pray with the patient for Jesus to heal the affliction. Several years ago, my sister came down with pneumonia, which then progressed to a virulent staph infection. We immediately brought her to the hospital. That night the physician told us that she probably wouldn't live through the night. But we also prayed for her healing—and she survived. Later her physician said that he didn't know of anyone else her age (she was seventy-seven) who had survived such a serious infection.

Nearly all of us have had to face sickness and accidents that threaten our lives or, at the very least, put us out of action for awhile. In these times, we can turn to prayer. Praying should be as normal and as immediate as calling the doctor. In fact, praying to heal the sick is an ancient Catholic practice. Along with the editors of *The Word Among Us*, I want this book to encourage you to take part in restoring this traditional practice. It is truly *good news* to know that our Lord Jesus Christ still heals the sick when we ask him.

It was forty years ago, when I was in my early forties, that I first learned this exciting truth, and it continues to affect my life in a marvelous way. I hope that you also have already discovered for yourself what I learned back then. Unfortunately, however, many Catholics have not yet discovered and experienced what is truly a large part of our Christian—our Catholic—inheritance.

Of course, we Catholics have a long tradition of praying *for* the sick (usually at a distance), but most of us have never learned to pray *with* a sick person, nor do we often have a strong expectancy that the person will get well because of our prayers. Discovering that Jesus helps us in the painful situations we will all face can lift terrible burdens from our hearts. If your child is severely injured in a bicycle accident or your spouse is diagnosed with cancer, knowing how to pray for healing can be a life-and-death issue. At least three times in her life, my wife, Judith, was restored to health through prayer.

We are not just talking about a special, unusual spirituality here. We are talking about how Jesus can help us in our ordinary, everyday lives. If you are not accustomed to regularly praying for the sick, this book is meant to encourage you to learn how to do so. Once you begin, I believe that your life will be transformed by what you see happening. To me, discovering this secret has been like discovering the treasure that Jesus describes in his story about the merchant who sold everything he had in order to buy the field where the treasure was hidden (Matthew 13:44). The field is the Church; the treasure has been there all along, but most people still don't realize that healing power is in the Church and is part of their inheritance. Once you find this treasure, your life will never be the same.

To encourage you, let me share just one testimony from a recent conference:

> It's been nearly four months since my experience, and life continues to be vastly different. I have a hunger and thirst for God that I never had before. . . . No matter what I'm doing, I feel Him with me, walking beside me in a tangibly personal way. . . .
>
> My long struggle with lust and pornography is nearly gone and is drastically different than it was before. The hole that I was attempting to fill with those sins is no longer there—it has been filled with God's Spirit. It hasn't been a perfect four months, as I still fail on occasion, but it is markedly different. . . .
>
> I have been finding a whole different aspect of my spirituality in the Catholic Church and find a new passion for the sacraments that I never knew.

... I have been much more outgoing in meeting new people. This has led me to a rescue mission, where I have the opportunity to work with the homeless. This is spiritually exhausting but very rewarding. It's amazing to see how much a handshake or a pair of socks means to these desperate people. ...

My prayer life has been energized with power and results. I've had numerous examples already of answered prayer—regarding healing, deliverance from oppressive spirits, and relational problems.

There is much more to my friend's moving story, but it shows that healing prayer is usually deeper than just asking for help to cure a physical, bodily sickness—important as that is. Healing can and should involve a wonderful transformation on every level of our being.

In this book, I'll talk about why we pray for healing and its basis in Scripture and our Catholic tradition. I'll also discuss some of the common obstacles we face in learning how to pray with others for healing. This book will also show you how to pray for healing, and the different types of healing prayer that are available to you. In addition, I'll address the healing effects of the sacraments and the use of sacramentals in healing prayer, as well as the connection between medicine and prayer.

Finally, a little bit about my own background. I am a cradle Catholic and was ordained a Dominican priest in 1956. In 1967 I experienced the baptism in the Holy

Spirit and began praying for the sick, many of whom were healed or noticeably improved. More and more I realized that a very important part of Jesus' ministry—healing and deliverance through the power of the Holy Spirit—had been commonplace in the early Church but had been largely overlooked or ignored in the modern Church. I soon became involved full-time in giving conferences and talks on the Holy Spirit and healing prayer. Over the years I have traveled to thirty-one countries on all five continents, speaking to thousands of Catholics about the need for the power of the Spirit in their lives.

My life took another turn in 1975 when I met Judith Sewell, a missionary in Jerusalem. In 1980, after consultation, we decided to marry. I immediately sought a dispensation from the Church, and in 1993 it was granted, and we renewed our marriage vows in the presence of then Bishop John Snyder of St. Augustine, Florida. In November 2001, Judith and I traveled to Rome at the invitation of Cardinal James Stafford, then president of the Pontifical Council for the Laity, to take part in an international colloquium in Rome for one hundred and fifty participants on the topic of the charism of healing. Since then we've had the wonderful opportunity of hosting two international five-day conferences on healing in Jacksonville, Florida, cosponsored by the International Catholic Charismatic Renewal Services (ICCRS), an organization that coordinates the Catholic Charismatic Renewal worldwide and is recognized by the Vatican's Pontifical Council on the Laity.

At the 2008 conference, participants came from thirty-seven different countries. Judith and I now direct Christian Healing Ministries in Jacksonville, Florida, where thousands of people come each year to get prayed with for healing and to receive teaching on how to pray effectively for healing.

Healing prayer has changed my life. Now I encourage you to embark on this wonderful journey of transformation and experience for yourself the truth of what Jesus has promised: "If you, then, evil as you are, know how to give your children what is good, how much more will your Father in heaven give good things to those who ask him!" (Matthew 7:11).

Come, then, with me and unearth the treasure in the field just waiting for you to discover. The lives of your family and friends may depend on it!

Francis MacNutt, PhD

ONE

WHY WE PRAY
FOR THE SICK

P rayer for healing depends upon the gift of faith. We need to believe that God has the power to heal through our prayers. But just as having the gift of faith is important, it is also important for us to have a reasonable foundation upon which to base our healing practice. I believe we can base our healing prayer on Scripture, tradition, and our own human experience.

- Sacred Scripture encourages us to pray for healing.
- Catholic tradition also encourages us to pray.
- Our human experience backs up our belief in the effectiveness of healing prayer with real evidence of healing that actually happens when we pray.

SACRED SCRIPTURE

Over and over in the gospels, we read that Jesus encouraged his followers to pray with expectant faith for the sick. When we read the New Testament, we become aware of how great a part healing prayer plays in the gospel story. St. Luke, in particular, tells us all kinds of healing stories.

Right at the beginning of Luke, we read how the archangel Gabriel appeared to Mary and told her that she must name her son Jesus (Luke 1:31) because his very name means "God heals" or "God saves." Jesus was his only name and was meant to signify his mission in life. ("Christ"—meaning the "anointed one"—is his title and not his last name.) And so, whenever we say the name of

Jesus, we are reaffirming our belief that his primary mission is to heal us.

When Jesus first began his public ministry, he stood up in the synagogue of his hometown of Nazareth and began reading from the prophet Isaiah and then applied the prophecy to himself:

> . . . he has anointed me
>   to bring the good news to the afflicted.
> He has sent me to proclaim liberty to captives,
>   sight to the blind
> to let the oppressed go free,
>   to proclaim a year of favour from the Lord.
>   (Luke 4:18-19)

Immediately after proclaiming these words, Jesus acted on them by going out and actually healing the sick and casting out evil spirits:

> At sunset all those who had friends suffering from diseases of one kind or another brought them to him, and laying his hands on each he cured them. (Luke 4:40)

Then Luke tells us many individual stories describing how Jesus healed the sick. As a result of people witnessing his healing powers, Jesus is overwhelmed by the crowds of suffering people who are chasing after him. Moved by compassion, he tells his followers to pray to the "Lord of the harvest to send out laborers to his harvest" (Matthew 9:37). Jesus needs help!

A little later, however, Jesus answers his own prayer for help by choosing the twelve apostles, with whom he shares his very own mission by bestowing on them his divine power and authority to cure disease (Luke 9:1). These simple, uneducated followers then set out and, two by two, go from "village to village proclaiming the good news and healing everywhere" (9:6).

Notice how significant this commissioning was: Jesus did not emphasize how different he was from us but instead shared the very same extraordinary divine power he possessed with ordinary people. His followers were not priests or scholars or elders; they were the blue-collar workers of his day, as it were.

We may be tempted to think: "St. Peter and the other apostles were the founders of the Church, and they are out of my league." The twelve apostles were unique, but that's no excuse for us to avoid healing the sick ourselves. In fact, in the very next chapter, Jesus chooses another seventy-two followers, whose names we don't even know, and tells them also to cure the sick:

> Whenever you go into a town where they make you welcome, eat what is set before you. Cure those in it who are sick, and say, "The kingdom of God is very near to you." (Luke 10:8-9)

Everything in the gospels encourages us—even orders us—to pray for the sick. Here are Jesus' own words:

> Until now you have not asked anything in my name. Ask and you will receive, and so your joy will be complete. (John 16:24)

It is truly astounding that whenever the sick approach Jesus and ask for healing, Jesus responds by making them well. We have no record of Jesus ever refusing to heal someone.

The extraordinary thing is that Jesus is never recorded as having told a sick person (as we might be tempted to do) that God was testing that person in order to teach him patience. Instead, we always read that Jesus healed the one who asked. Sickness is not seen as a blessing in disguise but as a curse. The gospels encourage us to pray for sickness to go away.

Jesus talks about the way human parents feel when their children are sick: "Is there anyone among you who would hand his son a stone when he asked for bread?" (Matthew 7:9) As a human father, I know that I want my children to get well when they are sick and suffering. I still remember when our children would fall seriously ill. We would get up in the middle of the night, I would put the child in Judith's arms, and we would immediately drive to the nearest hospital. Here Jesus is saying, "How much *more* will your Father in heaven" bless you when you ask

(7:11, emphasis added). God is far more loving than any parent. He is not going to put coal in our stocking.

The Book of Acts describes the early history of the Church and shows that after Jesus' death and resurrection, the Church continued his healing mission. God continued to work miracles because the Church was simply Jesus continuing his healing work, only now it was multiplied by thousands of Christians, and through them—and through us—Jesus is still healing the sick.

> It happened that Publius' father was in bed, suffering from fever and dysentery. Paul went in to see him, and after a prayer he laid his hands on the man and healed him. When this happened, the other sick people on the island also came and were cured. (Acts 28:8-9)

It is only in Acts and the letters of St. Paul that we read not only about the sick being healed but also about some Christians who were not healed. For instance, Paul talks about a revolting sickness that he himself suffered for some time:

> You have never been unfair to me; indeed you remember that it was an illness that first gave me the opportunity to preach the gospel to you, but though my illness was a trial to you, you did not show any distaste or revulsion; instead, you welcomed me as

a messenger of God, as if I were Christ Jesus himself. (Galatians 4:12-14)

And then there is Paul's famous "thorn in the flesh":

Wherefore, so that I should not get above myself, I was given a thorn in the flesh, a messenger from Satan to batter me and prevent me from getting above myself. About this, I have three times pleaded with the Lord that it might leave me; but he has answered me, "My grace is enough for you: for power is at full stretch in weakness." It is, then, about my weaknesses that I am happiest of all to boast, so that the power of Christ may rest upon me; and that is why I am glad of weaknesses, insults, constraints, persecutions and distress for Christ's sake. For it is when I am weak that I am strong. (2 Corinthians 12:7-10)

There is, by the way, no evidence here that the "thorn" was necessarily a disease or physical ailment. In the Old Testament, a thorn such as the one described in this passage refers to a wounding human relationship, and so this "thorn" could very well have been a person who drove Paul crazy. The key thing to note is that Paul automatically assumed that he was supposed to pray to get rid of the "thorn." It was only when it didn't disappear (after Paul had prayed three times to remove it) that he was puzzled, and so he prayed to find out what he was supposed to do next.

Then a few lines later, Paul defends his record as an apostle by calling our attention to the miracles that regularly follow his work: "All the marks characteristic of a true apostle have been at work among you: complete perseverance, signs, marvels, demonstrations of power" (2 Corinthians 12:12).

Paul boasts in long, passionate passages about his suffering, but he doesn't boast about his physical sickness, the kind of sickness that comes from the body's falling apart from within. If we follow Jesus, we know that we will certainly suffer, just as Jesus did. And yet we never think about him being sick, do we? Throughout the gospels, we are encouraged to pray for the sick as well as to visit them.

"If you ask me anything in my name, I will do it" (John 14:14). If we really believe this, how can we justify not praying to heal our sick brothers and sisters who suffer in our fallen world?

OUR CATHOLIC TRADITION

For some reason, Catholics have gotten the impression that praying for healing is a Protestant practice rather than its being at the very heart of our own tradition. To the contrary, the Protestant reformer (and founder of the Presbyterians), John Calvin, wanted to rid Europe of the Catholic healing shrines because he believed they were a a Catholic superstition. In general, most mainline Protestant denominations (such as Episcopalian, Baptist, and Presbyterian) do not teach healing prayer. This is also true for the largest Protestant denomination in the United States, the Southern Baptists. The healing services we often see on television are led mostly by independent Pentecostals, and most of our impressions of an active healing ministry have been formed by viewing such programs.

Back in the 1970s, I was interviewed on Australian TV and was asked, "Do you really think that a priest should be a 'faith healer'?" Being considered a "faith healer" usually implies that you are somehow a fraud, making money off the gullible. My response to the interviewer was that, to the contrary, I thought something had really gone wrong when a Catholic priest did not pray to heal the sick. "It goes with the territory," I added. We might ask in response whether Jesus himself should be considered a "faith healer."

But now, thanks be to God, we are seeing the beginnings of a great change throughout the United States and the world. We now see some priests who pray for healing and who are known for conducting healing services, usually connected with a celebration of the Eucharist. Fifty years ago such healing Masses were unheard of.

What we Catholics are coming to realize is that praying for healing is an essential part of our own tradition and goes way back—to the very beginning.[1]

For the first 350 years, the leaders of the early Church taught that every Christian could heal the sick and even cast out evil spirits. For example, Tertullian (around A.D. 200), one of the early Fathers of the Church, asserted that if a man is possessed by an evil spirit, this demon "can be commanded *by any Christian at all*," and "they are forced to leave the bodies they have invaded" (emphasis added).[2]

In fact, Catholics have never lost their belief in healing prayer. Witness the crowds who travel to the famous shrine in Lourdes (at the foot of the Pyrenees Mountains in France) where thousands of people still come every day during the summer, at a time when France is now largely secular, or in the United States, where devout believers still attend novenas in their parish churches. Nevertheless, three key elements have been greatly diminished:

1. People no longer have an *expectant* faith that leads them to believe that they will see astounding healings when they themselves pray.

2. They have also lost the confidence that *anyone* can pray for healing—not just holy people or priests.

3. When they do pray for the sick, it is usually at a distance and not *with* the sick person, with the laying on of hands.

The Way We Were

The earliest tradition of the Church taught that the best way to convert pagans was by healing them and casting out evil spirits. This goes back to Jesus' own example, when he sent out the Twelve to preach and also commanded them to heal the sick and cast out evil spirits:

He summoned his twelve disciples and gave them authority over unclean spirits with power to drive them out and to cure all kinds of disease and all kinds of illness. . . . "And as you go, proclaim that the kingdom of Heaven is close at hand. Cure the sick, raise the dead, cleanse those suffering from virulent skin-diseases, drive out devils. You received without charge, give without charge." (Matthew 10:1, 7-8)

Notice that Jesus' primary motive was simply *compassion*, because he saw that the ordinary people of his day were "harassed and dejected, like sheep without a shepherd" (Matthew 9:36).

The traditional understanding of this passage is that our world is under the dominion of evil and that Jesus came to save us—that is, to take the world back from the kingdom of Satan and transform it (and us, especially) into a "new creation" (2 Corinthians 5:17). Jesus' basic message was that the kingdom of God is now here.

The corollary is that the kingdom of Satan, of evil, is now at an end. Jesus healed the sick to show in a dramatic way that the ancient curse of sickness was coming to an end.

In those first 350 years, the Christian boast was that *any ordinary* Christian could heal the sick, while pagans could not. Many Christians were illiterate and from the lower classes; they were not converted by profound arguments about doctrine. Christians were persecuted and at times killed, so they were not able to organize large meetings to hear famous evangelists preaching in coliseums. Most conversions took place privately when neighbors told *their* neighbors that the Christian God was the only God and that they could test it out by asking Jesus to heal the sick. Christians regarded the pagan gods as demonstrably weak; they thought of them as false gods or even demons.

This simple conversion technique that reached simple, uneducated people reminds us of a typical Western movie featuring the classic shoot-out on Main Street, in which the heroes and villains confront each other and fire away until all the villains are destroyed. Seen in simple terms, the contest is a power encounter between good and evil, not just an intellectual discussion.

It was only in the fourth century, after the emperor Constantine was converted in 312, that miraculous healing came to be regarded as a rare outcome of prayer. Once Christianity became sanctioned by the state and grew in popularity, people gradually started believing that only those who were exceptionally holy could heal the sick, namely saints and priests.

For the next thousand years, the Church still maintained a lively but limited belief in healing prayer. The histories of the saints in the Middle Ages contain many stories about how God's love healed the sick through the prayers of these holy people. For example, I recently learned about a saint whom I had never previously heard of, St. Gregory Makar (c. 1010), who was "known for his holiness and for the miraculous cures of the sick wrought through his prayers. . . . The people . . . learned of his sanctity and received from him prudent counsel and miraculous cures."[3] Almost all of the famous saints healed the sick. When he was an old man, St. Anthony of the desert (c. 251–356) only had to touch people to heal them.

We can say that from about the year 400 through the Middle Ages (about a thousand years!), Catholics delighted in hearing about the miracles of God's healing power. How many of these stories are historically accurate is unknown, since some may have been pious stories meant to glorify God when scientific accuracy was not viewed as essential. However, in France the celebrated Dominican preacher St. Vincent Ferrer (1350–1419) was estimated to have worked 3,000 miracles, of which 873 were documented by the Church when he was canonized![4]

So although throughout the Middle Ages the people retained a lively belief in healing prayer, there was also a problem: Now only saints were viewed as being blessed by God with healing power. Ordinary laypeople had no confidence that they could pray to heal the sick; no humble person would be so vain as to presume that he was a "saint" and could pray for the sick and expect that healing would really happen.

Still later, during the Age of Reason and the Enlightenment beginning in the sixteenth and seventeenth centuries, faith in divine healing diminished drastically. When the scientific revolution swept Europe, anything that could not be measured or scientifically proven was subjected to methodical doubt: If you couldn't see it or measure it, it probably didn't exist. Another casualty among traditional religious beliefs was a universal belief in the existence of angels, including, of course, fallen angels or demons.

At this time there developed two different and conflicting views in the Church. On one level was popular belief, in which ordinary people still maintained their traditional devotions. They sought healing at Marian shrines, honored their guardian angels, and prayed to St. Michael for protection against Satan.

But there was another view to which many theologians and intellectuals adhered—a more sophisticated, agnostic approach. These intellectuals now began to teach that healing prayer and exorcism were superstitions that represented a primitive approach to religion. While thousands of simple people might journey to Lourdes every day, prayer for healing was not a topic considered worthy of theological study or for teaching at a seminary level. Those who held the opposing viewpoint usually didn't attack the other; they just ignored it.

These two different ways of thinking about miracles and healing are still with us. For example, on a popular level, people pray novenas and ask for the intercession of the Blessed Virgin Mary and saints such as St. Jude for their practical human needs, such as getting well or getting a job. Coexisting with what some would consider this "folk" religion is the other view, in which some scholars, on a quest for the "historical Jesus," not only question the literal reality of Jesus' healing miracles, but even the greatest miracle of all, his resurrection from the dead. If you question whether Jesus really performed physical healings, what's to stop you from questioning the most amazing miracle of all, the resurrection? The official teachings of the Church, especially those of the popes, continue to affirm the ancient beliefs. For example, Pope Paul VI reaffirmed a belief in the spiritual world of demons and even suggested that we study spiritual warfare in greater depth.[5]

This was the state of the Catholic world into which most of us were born, an environment in which we never learned to believe that our own prayers for healing might have an extraordinary, transforming effect and that beyond our words, even *our touch* might heal the sick. In the last forty years, however, we are seeing a great reversal of this view and a great increase in the number of Catholics who have once again learned to pray with confidence for healing.

We still have a long way to go. If we ever learn to pray for the sick with confidence, I believe that a gentle revolution will take place. Many of you will then see extraordinary miracles of healing—and your life and your family will be transformed!

Our Human Experience of Healing Prayer

The sick often get well when we pray. But if you've never prayed to heal someone who is sick, it can be difficult to begin. You might wonder if anything will really happen. You might question why you should take the chance. You might ask yourself, "Will I look foolish?" The simplest, most human answer I can give you is that healing prayer *works*. The sick who are prayed with often do get healed—or improve.

And yet most Catholics don't know this wonderful truth. And it's truly tragic that so many don't realize how much of our healing heritage we have lost. For example, when I've preached in Catholic churches, I've had the opportunity to ask for a show of hands when I pose this question: "How many of you can remember your father ever praying *with* you for your healing when you were sick as a child?" The startling answer is that only about three percent, on average, could remember their fathers ever praying with them! Mothers are usually more faithful in praying, but even so, only about 20 percent can remember their mothers ever praying with them when they were ill. And I have asked this question of thousands of parishioners, so it's not a small sample. (If you are a priest or pastor, you might ask the same question of the people in your church and see what their responses are.) It seems that most mothers and fathers have prayed *for* (but not *with*) their children when they are sick, but usually without much faith that the child will really be healed.

And so the simplest human reason that we should learn to pray for the sick is that they are often healed when we pray. Nevertheless, most people probably need encouragement to begin praying for and *with* the sick. Above all, you're probably not sure that anything will happen if you pray. We are all hesitant to try something new, especially because none of us likes to look foolish. Most of us pray for the first time when several things happen simultaneously to push us to take the risk and try:

1. You find out that the *true tradition* of the Church encourages you as an ordinary layperson to pray for the sick; therefore, you decide that perhaps you *ought* to pray.

2. Someone you *know and love* is desperately ill, and his or her only hope is for you to pray that God will heal him or her. (For instance, someone in your family develops stage-four cancer, and the doctors offer no hope for a medical cure.)

3. You're the only one available to pray (or you join a team that is going to pray).

And so, in desperation you try it! You have nothing to lose and everything to gain. But you don't have to be desperate to start. It makes more sense to begin praying with someone if there is a less serious problem—for example, a family member comes home with a sprained wrist.

For your encouragement, I want to share my own experience (and that of countless others) that God really does answer prayer. If you learn that perhaps God really will heal someone you love, then you begin to develop an *expectant* faith. Finally, you decide to launch out and pray. Then, see what happens!

With over forty years of experience, I've seen thousands of sick people at least get better when we pray, and some are totally healed. The most extraordinary thing of all is how much healing takes place. Once you actually see what happens to bless your family and friends when you pray, your life (and your family's life) will never be the same.

Most of us seem to go through two stages in our personal history of healing prayer. At first, we have little or no belief that anything will happen when we pray for the sick. Then, when we find out how much happens when we pray, we begin to wonder why it doesn't always happen! Yet not everybody we pray for seems to receive healing, and this is a great mystery, which we will never be able to adequately explain with our human reason.

However, suppose a new cancer treatment came on the scene that cured even 10 percent of patients. No one would say that the new drug should not be made available because 90 percent of the patients would be devastated if they didn't get well. Instead, people would rush out to get the new drug or even travel down to Mexico to get treatment. Terminal cancer patients would be greatly encouraged to think that they might be among the group who would be cured. A realistic *hope* is all that is required!

We do hear about reputable Christian leaders who have never had the experience of seeing people get well through prayer, and they want to discourage what they see as the building up of false hopes. We try to be very honest in our expectant faith, and we do not promise that everyone we pray for will get well.

But at Christian Healing Ministries, we pray for thousands of people, and our goal is for some—even many—to get better or totally well. And we find that even when they are not physically healed, they are encouraged by the group (or person) who prays for them, and

WHY WE PRAY FOR THE SICK

they actually experience a sense of the presence of the God who loves them. After the typical small healing service that we hold here in Jacksonville, Florida, the people we are praying with often don't want to leave right after we finish because they feel the lingering comfort of God's presence. And this is the usual, ordinary response of the people who come here.

It reminds us of St. Peter's response after Jesus' transfiguration on the mountain: "Let's build three tents" (see Matthew 17:2-4). After he was visited by Moses and Elijah, he didn't want them to leave. That's been our experience: After we pray, everyone experiences the presence of Jesus, and they feel like staying and pitching their tents.

What to Expect When You Pray

Most of the time when I have been with a group praying to heal a bodily sickness, I have seen a visible change take place. This is definitely "good news," and if every Catholic realized this truth and acted on it, our broken world would begin to heal.

I believe that some of these wonderful blessings will take place when any ordinary Catholic prays. St. Paul mentions that some Christians have special "gifts of healing" (1 Corinthians 12:9), but I believe that *all* of us are meant to pray for healing. Paul is simply pointing out that some people are especially gifted—when they pray, even more healing takes place. I like to compare this to people who are athletically gifted. All of us can walk (unless we have a physical impairment), but some are faster runners than the rest of us, and they may end up running in the Olympics. I had a first cousin who won a bronze medal fifty years ago hurdling in the Olympics, but that didn't discourage me—or anybody else—from hiking and jogging on a regular basis; he was just stronger and faster than the rest of us. Similarly, when we know someone who seems to have a special gift of healing, we should be encouraged to learn to pray the best we can.

And yet, even after seeing that actual physical changes take place in most of the people we pray for, it also seems true that most of these people are not totally healed—but they are *improved*. That in itself is wonderful. Sick people usually seem to get better when we pray, and that can range from a small improvement of about 10 percent all the way up to perhaps 90 percent. For example, our son, David, injured his right shoulder, and so we spent about fifteen minutes praying with him. At the end of that time, he was moving his arm more freely and with much less pain. I believe that if only we had the chance to pray *longer* with those who are improved, some of them might be totally healed.

Many people seem to think in terms of "all or nothing," and this dramatic impression is emphasized on TV and at large healing services featuring people who take the platform and testify to their instant and total healing. This is wonderful, and it's certainly the way you would like to see things happen—totally, dramatically, and instantaneously. And sometimes it does happen that way. But with the vast majority of people out there in real life, in the church or in the stadium (or at home), that's not the way it is.

For our part, what we need is total honesty and a desire to help all the sick for whom we pray. Leading a healing service or being the priest celebrating a healing Mass is an unusual opportunity that most of us don't have, but those of us who learn to pray at home or with friends may actually have a better chance of seeing someone we love be healed.

Three Stages of Healing

When physical healing does take place, it usually happens in stages. Here are some things to look for when you are praying:

1. *Pain.* With an illness, there is usually pain involved; but as you pray, the pain usually decreases, and often it totally disappears, even when the condition, such as cancer, remains.

2. *Motion.* When the infirmity has resulted in impaired movement, after extended prayer you may observe that the mobility of the injured part returns. For example, if you pray for someone who has arthritic fingers that

no longer bend enough to touch the hand, these frozen fingers start to bend until gradually their full range of motion is restored. This usually doesn't start to happen until after you have been praying for a while.

3. *Structure*. Prayer can change the actual structure of the bodily injuries, healing physical deformity. Going back to the example of arthritis, if the fingers have been bent out of shape for many years, you may see them actually start to straighten. This marvelous change usually takes much more time, and yet we have often seen it happen immediately!

Large healing services, taking place during a limited time, are not the best model to show us how we can pray in the most effective way at home (or at work) for the sick. What we need is a way to encourage ordinary people to pray with their families or friends.

Jesus spoke of the *works* he had done (John 15:24), rather than about his miracles, because I think he wanted to emphasize that they are ordinary (his "works") rather than emphasizing the miraculous element. In this book, my intention is not to get you to hold a healing service or anything that ambitious. I simply want to encourage you to pray with your family, friends, or those at work in a kind of ordinary way, when someone has a health problem. We want to pull healing prayer out of the realm of the extraordinary and make it as ordinary for Catholics as praying the Rosary.

The results of this type of prayer, however, may be extraordinary. And you may be like the seventy-two disciples who came back excited after having been sent out by Jesus to heal the sick. Jesus said to them, "For I tell you that many prophets and kings wanted to see what you see, and never saw it; to hear what you hear, and never heard it" (Luke 10:24).

TWO

Overcoming
Our Prejudices

If what I have said so far is true—namely, that healing prayer is an essential part of the gospel message and that God wants *all* of us to pray for the sick—then we have to account for the near death of healing prayer in the Church. How can it be that in the early Church (the first 350 years), everyone prayed for the sick, but today most of us can't remember even our mothers or fathers praying with us when we were sick as children?

Clearly, people today see things differently. Where did this doubt and disbelief enter in?

In this section, I will share two common beliefs or prejudices that act as roadblocks that prevent us from praying for healing. These thought patterns have been prevalent for hundreds of years and have quietly robbed the Church of its glorious heritage of healing prayer.

Catholics have grown up with two strong excuses for not praying to heal the sick:

1. "Only *saints* can expect to work miracles, and I'm no saint."

2. "I don't have the kind of *faith* that is needed to pray for healing."

I hope this chapter will eliminate these prejudices, which stand in the way of our praying to heal the sick. It's significant that the word used for "repent" in the gospels is *metanoia*, which means a *change of attitude*.

That's exactly what we're talking about here: a change in our world view!

"BUT I'M NO SAINT!"

As we have said, the early tradition was that any Christian could—and should—pray for healing. But once Christianity became more widely accepted (A.D. 350), healings were less common, and enthusiasm and fervor died out. Those Christians who were trying to live holy lives often decided that they had to flee the sinful cities, where it was hard to avoid the contamination of a lax Christianity or a pagan society.

In the fourth century, some Christians fled the cities (such as the capital of Constantinople) by escaping into the desert to do penance and pray in solitude. Later they were joined by other like-minded Christians, and together they built monasteries where they could live in community. They came to be honored as the "desert fathers." In the wilderness they sought humility and poverty—a stark contrast to the wealth and extravagance they had witnessed in the cities.

Soon people came flocking to the wilderness to be taught by these holy monks and to seek their prayers for healing. The monks, however, intent on personal holiness, were worried that people would idolize them, and so they usually refused to pray, but instead, encouraged the sick to visit the shrines dedicated to saints. (The saints in heaven were beyond being affected by praise, so it was acceptable to seek their intercession.)

In a short time, very few Christians felt worthy to pray in person for the sick for fear that others would put them on a pedestal and consider them extraordinary and holy. It was a no-win situation: If any person was truly a saint, he or she would not presume to pray for healing because that would be like saying, "I think I'm a saint." And so anyone who was saintly would simply refuse to pray!

We can certainly appreciate the cautious and humble approach of these monks, who were striving above all things to be holy. They took Jesus' warning seriously about being a hypocrite who loves to pray in public (Matthew 6:5-6). However, sick people would just ignore the monks' refusal to pray by imitating the woman with the issue of blood in the gospel story, when she boldly went ahead and touched the hem of Jesus' garment (Mark 5:27). The most celebrated desert father of all, St. Anthony, was famous for healing those who merely touched him, although he would usually refuse to say a prayer for healing. While the humility of these monks is admirable, it also meant that ordinary Christians no longer prayed for the sick to be healed.

This hands-off attitude influenced the entire Church, so much so that sixteen hundred years later, a month after my ordination, I refused when a Protestant friend asked me to pray for his partially blind son to recover his sight.

Since I didn't see myself as a saint, I just didn't believe that anything physical would happen when I prayed. And I didn't want to disappoint my friend—or myself. So I refused to pray.

Also, since no one else I knew was praying to heal the sick, I was afraid that I would stand out as some kind of religious eccentric. It wouldn't be surprising if you have experienced some of these same fears of public opinion. After honestly confronting his own fears, one of my friends said that faith should be spelled R-I-S-K. He is right. There are two great risks we must all face when we pray for healing. One is that the person *will not* be healed, and you will look foolish. The other is that the sick person *will be* healed, and you will become known as a fanatic or as a "faith healer"! Either way, you are caught! (Along these lines, one of my priest friends once remarked, "I'm so glad I'm not Frank MacNutt, who has all those crowds of sick people chasing after him!")

An Encouraging Gospel

And yet the gospel is very clear that we should—all of us—be praying for the sick. To take just one passage, in the last chapter of Mark, Jesus is quoted as saying, "These are the signs that will be associated with believers: in my name they will cast out devils; . . . they will lay their hands on the sick, who will recover." (Mark 16:17,

18). Notice that Jesus doesn't say that these signs will follow those who are *saints* but rather, those who are simply *believers*.

I already mentioned how Jesus told the Twelve that they should preach that the kingdom of God had come to this earth. Then, to make the kingdom a reality, he also commanded them to heal the sick and cast out evil spirits. Our temptation may be to say that the Twelve were special—they were the apostles, and we even know their names. But as we pointed out earlier, for the next mission, Jesus chose *seventy-two* disciples whose names we don't know and also commissioned them to heal the sick (Luke 10:1, 9). These seventy-two nameless disciples represent us: ordinary Catholics who are told to preach that God's kingdom is here as well as to heal the sick.

As I have already noted, for the first 350 years, Christians took the command to heal the sick and cast out evil spirits very seriously and believed that any Christian could do these things, even those who were not ordained. Because Christians were persecuted in those early days, they did not hold large public meetings, and they had very few famous preachers. Churches, as we think of them, came into existence only after the conversion in 312 of the emperor Constantine, who then donated the pagan temple buildings for use as churches. Before that time, Christians met in homes and had to remain hidden.

So most conversions came about in people's homes as a result of *seeing* miracles of healing and deliverance.

For example, St. Gregory of Neocaesarea (who died in 268) worked so many miracles and was responsible for so many conversions to Christianity that he was called "the Wonderworker." It was said that when he started out, there were only seventeen Christians in his region, but at the end of his life, there were barely that many who were not Christian.[6]

The most shocking examples of how Christian healing was diminished and restricted were in England and France, where healing gradually became concentrated in the hands of kings and queens. In the Middle Ages, these monarchs were believed to have a special power (the "Royal Touch") to heal one particular disease, scrofula, which was called the "King's Disease."[7] When Charles I of England came to power in 1625, he even made it a crime for anyone else to pray for healing. By that time, bishops and priests were no longer praying to heal the sick, so they weren't the targets of the king's restrictive law. He was only trying to put out of business the folk healers, such as "the seventh sons of seven sons," who were supposed to have special powers to heal (they still are presumed to have such powers in some folk cultures).

Politically, it was advantageous for the kings and queens to hold healing services because their "healing touch" showed that they were the Lord's anointed, and so common folk would be foolish to revolt against them. For example, in France Louis XIV held a healing service for three thousand people on Pentecost Sunday 1698; again, it was dramatic proof that there was such a thing as the "divine right of kings."

In both England and France, the monarchs held healing services for hundreds of years. In England the practice can be traced back to Edward the Confessor (1003–1066) and in France to King Clovis I (c. 466–511). The Royal Touch continued until the Protestant German monarchs came to England in 1688. In France it ended with the French Revolution, when the Bourbon monarchs were beheaded by the guillotine.

In all of this, we see, amazingly, that there was still a lively belief in God's healing power. But it had been severely restricted to

- *Who* could pray for healing: only the monarchs, no one else.
- *What* could be healed: only scrofula, the King's Disease, not every type of ailment.
- *When* the healing could take place: at a special healing service once or twice a year.
- *Where* the healing could take place: at the one site that the monarchs decided on, not anywhere else.
- *Why* the healing took place: to prove that the kings and queens were divinely anointed, not primarily to manifest the compassion of God taking pity on wounded humanity.

At this point in time, the practice of healing prayer was being kept alive by the kings and queens; the Church now stood on the sidelines. And then even those healing practices died out, leaving a vacuum in the Christian churches in France and England. and in all of Europe, for that matter!

Now in the Catholic Church, we are living in an exciting time, when the ancient belief in healing prayer is experiencing a resurrection! When we pray for the sick, we no longer need to think of presuming that we are holy. We only need to have faith that Jesus can use ordinary Christians like ourselves (Paul calls ordinary believers like us "saints"; see 1 Corinthians 1:2, for example) to pray with faith to conquer sickness.

Fifty years ago, very few would presume to pray for healing, but now many (but not all) priests pray for healing. As a sign of this renewal, the International Catholic Charismatic Renewal Services (ICCRS) in Rome, which coordinates the Charismatic Renewal worldwide and is sponsored by the Vatican's Pontifical Council on the Laity, has convened conferences on healing prayer. One was held in Rome in 2003. Pope Benedict XVI has actively encouraged Catholics to be baptized in the Spirit and to rediscover and experience the charisms, including healing.[8]

Our ministry here in Jacksonville has had the privilege of cosponsoring two conferences with ICCRS. At these two conferences, seven hundred international Catholic leaders from forty-five countries traveled to the United

States, spending five days learning about healing prayer. This is truly a new day and takes us back to our spiritual roots. At the ICCRS conference we cosponsored here in Jacksonville from October 20–25, 2008, one third of the participants did not consider English their first language. Among the many powerful testimonies that we heard, the key word that stands out is "transformation." One participant testified, "I was inundated with miracles. I was crushed by miracles. I was reborn by miracles. I will never be the same again." Another participant wrote to say, "My right shoulder has had restricted motion and considerable pain for the past ten years. When the participants laid their hands on me, I was completely healed, and I can now do push-ups with no pain, and complete motion has been restored."

Nevertheless, most ordinary Catholics have not learned to pray confidently themselves one-on-one for healing. In our homes especially, we need to shake off the habits of a lifetime and learn about the wonders of what Jesus can do, with the understanding that we don't have to be saints to pray for healing. If you are an ordinary Catholic, you can truly hope to see miracles of healing take place—especially in your home with your family and friends.

God wants to use you to bring his kingdom into this world. "Thy kingdom come, / Thy will be done, / on *earth* as it is in heaven" (Matthew 6:10, RSV, emphasis added). You are being offered this marvelous, exciting mission to change the world and to bring heaven to earth.

A True Story

Here is an example of the kind of healing we regularly see. The following is a testimony from a good friend, Barbara Holmes of Wilmington, Delaware, and it will encourage you to begin praying for healing if you have not done so already:

I'm having trouble finding words to convey my thanks to you! When I arrived on Wednesday night at the conference, I was very sick. I was speaking in a weak, whispering voice and had serious weakness in my legs and feet. My healing began on Thursday, Francis, when you laid hands on my diaphragm and prayed for it to function properly so that I could regain my speech that had been barely audible for two and a half months. My ENT doctor and speech therapist had both said my diaphragm muscle was too weak. I did not even have the strength to blow a whistle! I appreciate your taking your prayers to Jesus for me. I hope you remember my first word— a loud and resounding "alleluia."

Then came Friday night when you, dear Judith, so graciously agreed to "take one more" person for prayer. How forever grateful I am that you said yes! You prayed for my weakened legs, feet, and hips as I lay on the floor. Before you prayed, Judith, I had been in the hospital for five days and was using a cane and a walker. I had been suddenly weakened by dystonia in both feet, and a remote and very rare virus had rendered my legs virtually useless.

For two and a half months, I could not even lift my legs one inch off the bed. I had been homebound with only visiting nurses, physical therapists, and speech therapists coming to me three times a week. I could not drive and could not walk very far, even inside my house. Getting up stairs was an extremely painful and slow process.

But when you prayed, Judith, within fifteen minutes I could lift my legs—both of them—one *inch* off the floor. After you "soaked" me in prayer for an additional half hour, I could finally lift both legs three *feet* off the floor! I knew God was healing me as you prayed for the basal ganglia in my brain. The electricity flowing through my head was intense and beautiful. I knew that God had healed me!

Immediately, walking became normal once again, and I tossed aside my cane, my walker, my shower seat, and my handicap sticker! They all now reside in my attic. I do not need them.

This healing happened about a year after another remarkable healing that Barbara experienced:

I wanted to share joyful healing news with you, Francis. Do you remember June 28, 2008, when I sat down in the empty chair next to you and asked you to pray for my right shoulder? You so graciously agreed to pray. I had been experiencing severe pain, and lack of strength and mobility for more than a year due to a partially torn rotator cuff and several other diagnoses made from my MRI. My surgery was scheduled for November 2008.

You gently laid your hand on my shoulder and began praying. Within five minutes, my horrendous pain was gone, and I could lift my arm straight up in the air, something I had been unable to do for over a year.

When I returned to my orthopedic surgeon four weeks later, I didn't tell him about my healing right away. He thoroughly examined my shoulder and stated in an amazed voice, "Your shoulder is now totally normal." I might add that my physical therapist was equally astonished, since he also found absolutely nothing wrong with my shoulder.

I cancelled my November 2008 surgery. It was no longer needed. And I give thanks and praise to our healer, Jesus. All the glory and praise be to Jesus Christ, my Lord, my Savior, and my Healer.

"I DON'T HAVE ENOUGH FAITH"

Fifty years ago, very few Catholics were encouraged to pray for healing—in fact, it was quite the opposite.

What we did almost reflexively when we heard that someone was sick was to pray for *patience* to endure and for peaceful *acceptance* of the sickness that God had sent our way to help us grow in perseverance and long-suffering.

And yet when we read the gospel stories about the life of Jesus, he challenges us over and over again to have the faith to pray for healing. We have mentioned the story about the woman who suffered for twelve years with a hemorrhage (Mark 5:25-34). Somehow she got it into her head that if she could just touch Jesus' cloak, she would be healed. Then she moved unnoticed into the crowd. According to Jewish custom, she was considered "unclean," and so she did not want to ask Jesus to touch her, because then he would have become unclean himself and would have had to take time off for a ritual purification.

At the very moment when she secretly touched his robe, Jesus felt the power that would heal her go out from him. But far from blaming her for breaking the law, Jesus said, "My daughter, . . . your faith has restored you to health" (Mark 5:34). In other words, it wasn't only the power in Jesus that healed her; the woman's faith also had something to do with her healing. Again and again we read that we need a strong faith if we expect results from our prayers. "If you have faith, everything you ask for in prayer you will receive" (Matthew 21:22).

Now, that's a real challenge!

Over the years I have known some Christian leaders who have come up with various explanations of precisely

faith" means. I also know sick people can be spir-
ᴵᵗly wounded when a respected leader tells them that
they will absolutely be healed if only they had faith. The
sick person tries to summon up faith, but then wonders,
"Does this mean that I have to be absolutely certain that
I will be healed right now through this prayer?"

For years I have wrestled with this question, and after
seeing thousands of sick people healed but then seeing
others—including dear friends—who were not healed, I
have come to some conclusions that I think you will find
very helpful.

1. As Catholics, we have a firm belief that God is on the
   side of *life* and of *health*.

Just as we delight in seeing our friends, parents, and
children in good health, God also delights in seeing members of his own mystical body healthy and full of life. As
St. Irenaeus said, "The glory of God is a human being
fully alive." (And Irenaeus lived back in those early years
shortly after the earthly life of Jesus, 125–202.)

When I pray, I am not *certain* that the person will be
healed, but I still have a lively expectancy (unless there is
some counterindication, such as the person being involved
in spiritualism).[9]

2. We also know that for all of us, there comes a time to
   die. As Christians, we realize this is not a tragic fate,

since death simply opens the door for a transition into a better, happier life of union with Jesus.

How well I remember my dear friend Tommy Tyson, who traveled with me giving retreats all around the world for thirty-five years. At least three times, I prayed with Tommy when he came down with a life-threatening illness, and each time he was amazingly healed. One time in Bolivia, he woke me up in the middle of the night, whispering that he was dying and wanted to go to confession. The next morning, after prayer, he was in perfect health.

But then when he was about eighty years old, he came down with a whole multitude of ailments, and it seemed fairly clear that now was the time for him to die, even though his family and friends would have liked to have kept him with them. When Tommy died, he spent his last words praising God.

An ancient tradition in the Church is that holy people—those close to God—somehow know a short time beforehand when they are going to die. Ordinarily, however, unless this is the case, I believe that we should all be encouraged to pray for life and health and healing.

3. There is a great *mystery* connected with healing prayer, and we don't know the outcomes of our prayers, unless God chooses to reveal to us exactly what those results will be.

For example, our daughter, Rachel, suffered from asthma for six years, and Judith and I faithfully prayed for her healing every day. Then one night at a healing service, two dear friends prayed for her, and she was healed. Why did it take six years? And why didn't it happen through *our* prayers? After all, we are her parents. More and more I realize that we are totally dependent on God, and more and more I tend to distrust anyone who claims to know for certain God's will at all times and in all situations. What I *am* sure about is that God loves us and that things work together for our good.

4. There are times, however, when God chooses to reveal to some people *how* he wishes them to pray, and occasionally he reveals that this particular person will be healed—and when.

What all of us would like is a map with definite directions and instructions. But God has not left us a printed map (which is under our control) but a personal, living *guide*—the Holy Spirit.

5. Faith involves an expectancy and a daring boldness.

I once consulted a noted Scripture scholar, Dr. Bob Lindsey, who had studied the gospels indepth, especially St. Mark, for forty-one years. During those years he worked with a Jewish rabbi in Jerusalem to discover what Jesus meant when he made certain statements and used certain words. And so when I had the chance to visit him, I asked him how Jesus himself, two thousand years ago, would have understood the word "faith."

Instantly he responded with the Yiddish word *chutzpah*, which is not so much about belief but means in our ordinary usage a kind of daring boldness—an attitude of "go for it." His example was the woman we mentioned earlier who had the issue of blood and who decided to touch Jesus, even though it was against the law. She dared to act and trust in God's goodness.

This understanding of faith has set me free, because now I don't have to pretend to know something, but I can just launch out in trust. My job is to pray, and it's up to God what happens as a result. My friends have always remarked (to my surprise) that I have great faith. But it doesn't seem that way to me; I don't feel that I have much faith at all, because when I pray, I usually don't know what's going to happen. I just pray with an "expectant" faith, looking forward to something happening, even though I'm not sure if the person will be healed. What I do believe is that God loves us and that he hears my prayer. In that I have absolute faith.

And that's what I encourage you to have. As a Christian—and as a Catholic—I believe that such an attitude is within your reach, assisted by grace. You can pray for the sick and truly expect God to work miracles through your prayers, even though you may not be sure how or when these wonders will happen!

Once you clear away these two prejudices, you can relax and pray for the sick:

- You don't have to be a "Saint" with a capital "S" to pray for healing. You just need to be a loving, ordinary Christian: a "saint" with a small "s."

•. You may not have certitude about what's going to happen when you pray. But you don't need to know! All you need to do is take the risk of praying for the sick: That's what faith is, and that much you can manage, with God's help.

The most loving attitude we can have toward our sick brothers and sisters is to take the risk of faith and pray for their healing. We all can do that much!

THREE

How to Pray
for Healing

By now I hope that even if you have never had the experience of praying with someone for healing, you are ready to give it a try—at least in your family. So where do you start? Having come this far, what do you do?

In our lives we experience—and in the gospels we read about—two very different but complementary channels through which healing prayer works:

- The word: the prayer that we say; and
- The touch: the laying on of hands.

More or less equal time is devoted to the topics of prayer and to the laying on of hands in the stories about Jesus and his followers, so we will now examine them and the benefits associated with each one.

The Word: The Prayer That We Say

Before we talk about the words we use to pray, let's first focus on our relationship with the Lord. Many of us have a relationship with God based on awe or fear. Some of us who grew up in the Church fifty years ago heard sermons about dying outside the state of grace, and our relationship with God was respectful but basically fearful.

This respectful relationship is where we begin, but Jesus in the gospels tells us, "I shall no longer call you servants. . . . I call you friends" (John 15:15). Even more amazing, Jesus says that he loves us as much as God the Father loves him (15:9). Can you really believe this? These statements are so strong, so powerful, and so beautiful that they're almost impossible for us to believe! As G. K. Chesterton once wrote, the gospel message is "too good to be true." The basis for our praying for healing is an extraordinary but true belief in how much God loves us and how much he also loves the sick person. This is the very foundation of our healing ministry, as Jesus makes clear: "If you remain in me and my words remain in you, you may ask for whatever you please and you will get it" (John 15:7).

When Jesus teaches his disciples how to pray in the famous prayer we all know by memory, the Our Father (Matthew 6:9-13), he also tells us that we can now address his Father as *our* Father. Scripture scholars say that the word that Jesus used for "Father" was "Abba." This is an affectionate term in Hebrew, and its closest translation is "Daddy." It's also a word that can only be used for your very own father. So Jesus is telling us that you are now a member of his very own family: Jesus is your brother, and his Father is your own dad. We would get some idea of the audacity and the boldness of calling God "Abba" if we taught people to say the Our Father by translating it (accurately) as "Our Dad, who is in heaven." This seems too personal—even irreverent. We know in faith that God loves us, but addressing him in this way goes way beyond the ordinary meaning of love; it places us in the very family of God.

The traditional Catholic belief in the Indwelling of the Trinity states that through baptism, the three Persons in One have come to make their home in us. If we believe that the Father, Son, and Holy Spirit live in us, then it's hard to justify our *not* praying for healing when one of our friends is sick.

Praying for healing is the ordinary, normal consequence of being a Christian. When our children were young and fell sick, we desperately wanted them to get well. Though it's hard for us to imagine, God tells us that his love is far greater than our human love for our children. If we really believe that God loves us, praying for the sick should seem the most natural thing in the world. Often when I pray, I think to myself, "I really want to see this child get well, but my desire to see this child well and happy again is nothing compared to the love that the Lord God himself has for this child."

The great prophet Isaiah put it this way:

Can a woman forget her baby at the breast,
 feel no pity for the child she has borne?
Even if these were to forget,
 I shall not forget you.
Look, I have engraved you on the palms of
 my hands. (Isaiah 49:15-16)

Young lovers carve their initials into the trunks of trees, and here is God going one step further, saying that he has carved us into the palms of his hands! And our Mother, Mary, has the biggest heart of anyone we will ever know, and we can ask her to intercede for the healing of our friends (and her children) too!

What Jesus encourages us to do is very easy—that is, simply to *ask* him to heal our sick friend. In the gospels we find no single way to pray. Each gospel story about healing is different, and I think this diversity is meant to show us that we aren't supposed to get locked into any one particular way of praying. One time Jesus made a mud cake and put it on a blind man's eyes and told him to go to a pool named Siloam and wash (John 9:6-7). Another time he put spit on a blind man's eyes and laid hands on them (Mark 8:22-26). I think Jesus knew that if he healed people the same way every time, we would imitate him and say, "This is the right way, the only way. Here's the prayer you have to say!"

Instead, we can make up our own prayers. Most of us grew up memorizing prayers such as the Our Father and the Hail Mary and never had the confidence to compose our own. I still remember the first time I heard someone pray spontaneously. It was at the first Cursillo retreat I ever attended (in Waterloo, Iowa, in the 1960s), and a burly truck driver came out with his own simple prayer. I was so deeply touched hearing an uneducated worker compose a heartfelt prayer that I had to hold back my tears. Since then, of course, more and more people have learned to pray in their own words, but many Catholics are still not used to the practice. In case you have never said a prayer for God to heal someone and you would like a model to get you started, here's an example of the kind of prayer you could say:

Dear Lord, we bring before you our friend Jim, who as you know is suffering from a broken wrist, and we ask that you send your healing power into his wrist to hasten the healing. Please take away the pain. And let your healing power and your love flow through our hands to heal him. We ask that any medications he is taking have the good effects intended by his doctors and that you block any possible harmful side effects. Help him sleep and rest at night. Let him know that you are a companion in his healing journey, and grant him the gift of patience. Lord, we thank you for your love for Jim and his family, and we ask that you be very present to all of them.

And Mary, our Mother, we ask you in a very special way to be here with us and intercede for Jim that he may be quickly restored to his family and to his work. [Here you might also say the Hail Mary.]

This is just one example of how you might compose a prayer that especially suits your ailing friend and his or her type of ailment.

We realize that not everyone we pray for is always physically (or spiritually) healed in the way we would like, but our job is to pray; the results are out of our hands. We need to be constantly aware of the mystery involved, especially as to why some people are healed and others are not. We usually don't know the answer.

And yet, as I said earlier, in the majority of cases, when we pray, some actual healing that we can observe seems to take place. I cannot encourage you enough to believe that often an answer to your prayer will be real and visible. As an example, I recently received an e-mail from a friend who has been in constant pain for three months from a rotator-cuff injury. Physicians performed surgery on her shoulder, but nothing had helped the pain. Last week we had a chance to pray with her, and three days later she wrote, "I cannot believe it! I have *no pain* in my shoulder for the first time since the surgery! I cannot tell you how happy I am. I am still not having a full range of motion, but incredibly I'm pain-free."

Practical Suggestions

Here are some practical suggestions that will help when you pray for the sick:

1. Be specific.

We have found that when we pray in a general way, not nearly as much seems to happen as when we are very specific in our request. For instance, if we pray "May God bless you," it does not seem nearly as effective as when we pray "Jesus, please send your healing power into this throat and clear away the infection and strengthen his or her immune system."

Sometimes we tend to make our prayers very vague because we lack the faith to be specific. It's easier to pray "God bless you" than "Jesus, please send your healing power into this swollen knee to take away the pain and the swelling."

2. Leave out "*if* it be your will."

Usually when we put into the prayer an "if," it's because we doubt whether anything is going to happen and we want to protect ourselves from going too far out on a limb. And yet it is true that *all* of our prayers depend upon God's will. You certainly can put in "if it be God's will" if that doesn't mean "I really don't think anything is going to happen."

3. Express your gratitude.

Be sure to include a thank-you to God for hearing and answering your prayer. Being grateful is based on our faith that God does really hear—and answers in some way—all our prayers.

Your prayers do not need to be eloquent, but they should be heartfelt. Once when our children were young, our son, David, prayed for me when I had a cold. "God, please heal my dad so that we can play baseball," he prayed, and then he added, "Get up, Dad!" Now, that was a not-so-eloquent but heartfelt prayer!

Most of us need encouragement to pray for healing and to get over the idea that healing prayer is a very special and holy activity only suited for very unusual people. When we read the life of Jesus in the gospels, what comes through over and over again is simply this: "Anything you ask from the Father he will grant in my name" (John 16:23). The love that Jesus has for you is the very basis of your healing abilities. We don't expect you to start by holding a healing service for hundreds of people; you can begin just by praying in private for your family and friends. So please try it!

TOUCH: THE LAYING ON OF HANDS

When we think about healing the sick, most of us automatically think of what prayer we will say. But nearly as much time is spent in the gospels describing how sick people get well through the healing power that comes through our touch. And so touch, or "the laying on of hands," is the other channel for God's healing power.

The last chapter of the Gospel of Mark says, "These are the signs that will be associated with believers: in my name they will cast out devils; they will have the gift of tongues; . . . they will lay their hands on the sick, who will recover" (16:17, 18). If I had been the author of this passage, I would probably have written, "They will *pray for* the sick who will recover." Instead, laying hands on the sick is what Mark mentions. Clearly, Mark had a lively sense of what might happen when we simply lay our hands on the sick.

Perhaps the most famous example of healing touch is the passage we have mentioned that describes the woman with the issue of blood who just touches the hem of Jesus' garment, believing that this simple touch will heal her (Luke 8:43-48). Jesus senses that power has gone out from him, so he turns to the crowd to ask, "Who was it that touched me?" Peter explains, "Master, it is the crowds round you, pushing" (8:45). But Jesus responds that he felt power go out from him, even though he hadn't said a prayer for her. It was just the power of his touch that healed the woman.

Encouraged by the gospels, we have learned that the ideal method of praying for the sick is to combine a spoken prayer for healing with the laying of hands on the sick person. Since some people are uncomfortable when others touch them, we always respect their desire for privacy by asking, "Would it be all right if we put our hands on your shoulders while we pray?" (or "on your head" or "hold your hands"). If it is an appropriate site, it is usually best to place our hands near the ailing part of the human body. For example, if the person has a sprained ankle, you might place your hands gently around the ankle.

An amazing thing is that usually we feel *heat* generated when we touch the person, and we have come to associate this heat with the body's response to God's healing power. In addition to the healing power that seems to flow, people also respond to the care and love shown when a group gathers around to pray for them.

I have often wondered where this power and heat come from, and I associate it with the traditional Catholic belief in the Indwelling of the Holy Trinity, by which we believe that through baptism, the Father, Son, and Holy Spirit are living within us. As Jesus said, "On that day you will know that I am in my Father and you in me and I in you" (John 14:20). At the Last Supper, Jesus told us that the Holy Spirit "is with you, he is in you" (14:17). It's such an awesome truth, but it's hard to believe that God lives in me; yet it's the constant teaching of the New Testament and our Catholic tradition.

And so I believe that when we reach out in prayer to touch a sick person, *Jesus himself*, in us, is also somehow reaching out through our hands to touch the sick person. I think you will find this true for yourself when you lay your hands on the sick; it's not only you, but Jesus truly is reaching out through you, and healing comes through his touch! In a sense, your hands are his hands!

SOAKING PRAYER

One of our greatest discoveries has been that if we really spend time with the sick, especially with the laying on of hands, the number of physical healings seems to greatly multiply. This is simply a deeper application of what we said earlier about usually observing improvement rather than total, instant healing. We have come to call this "soaking prayer," and it has become a popular practice in some Christian groups, with more and more people praying in this way.

We talked earlier about spending time with the sick. Our prayer—the words—can be simple, direct, and short. The spoken prayer may last only about three minutes. And yet your laying on of hands can continue on as long as you wish. The longer the affected part of the body is held in the field of God's love and power, the more that seems to happen. For example, we have seen instances in which the longer we prayed over a cancerous tumor, the more the growth seemed to grow *smaller* and *softer* while we prayed until, at last, the tumor was totally gone.

As we said, you don't have to say a long prayer, but while your laying on of hands continues, you can praise God, pray the Rosary, sing—or simply be quiet.

Recognize that it's the simple truth, not pride, that your touch can actually become like Jesus' touch to reach out and heal the sick. It's really very humbling to realize that something as simple as human touch can be used by

God to accomplish such an extraordinary thing as healing the sick!

Once you start to pray for healing, you will begin to discover many important things that you don't hear on TV or even read in books about God's healing gifts. Perhaps the most important thing that I learned was that bringing God's healing to a sick person often took *time*—a lot of time—and that most healing was not instant, although the impression you get if you watch TV is that it's all very dramatic and that it happens as you watch.

Instead, the healing sessions that I took part in often took hours, and we saw more people who improved than people who were totally healed in one prayer. For example, I had the privilege of praying for a woman who had stage-four ovarian cancer that, in a period of two years, had metastasized throughout her body and was now in her lungs, where it affected her breathing so much that she had to carry around a portable oxygen tank. Her joyful spirit and her positive hope in God were remarkable. We prayed with her for about half an hour, and at the end of that time, the crackling noise in her lungs had stopped. She was able to breathe more easily without wheezing. There was a definite change, a healing, but it was partial.

When she went a few days later to see her nurse for her regular appointment, the nurse was surprised and said that for the first time in two years, she could not detect any fluid in her lungs. To us, this improvement was a cause for great rejoicing, and we hoped that she was on her way to total healing, and so we all praised God.

But yet we could not say that she was now healed. We were in a battle for her life, and we had seen only a partial victory. Because there are so many people with cancer today, we are in a combat zone, and so we emulate Jesus by teaching other people—like you—how you can join in the army of Christians who pray for the sick.

We all appreciate whatever happens instantly (perhaps this is especially true of Americans), but the New Testament is very clear about the amount of time we may need in order for a healing to actually take place. The clearest text in the gospels on "soaking prayer" is in Luke, where Jesus describes an unjust judge who eventually answers the pleas of a poor widow who keeps on pestering him and demanding an answer to her prayers:

> Then he told them a parable about the need to pray continually and never lose heart. "There was a judge in a certain town," he said, "who had neither fear of God nor respect for anyone. In the same town there was also a widow who kept on coming to him and saying, 'I want justice from you against my enemy!' For a long time he refused, but at last he said to himself, 'Even though I have neither fear of God nor respect for any human person, I must give this

widow her just rights since she keeps pestering me, or she will come and slap me in the face.'"

And the Lord said, "You notice what the unjust judge has to say? Now, will not God see justice done to his elect if they keep calling to him day and night even though he still delays to help them? I promise you, he will see justice done to them, and done speedily. But when the Son of man comes, will he find any faith on earth?" (Luke 18:1-8)

The meaning of this passage is clear, and we notice that there are many references to the fact that we may need to spend a lengthy amount of time in prayer before we see any results. In fact, Jesus seems to be saying that faith itself consists in persisting in prayer, even when there seems to be no answer and we are tempted to "lose heart" (Luke 18:1). Of course, if it seemed that the prayer was being answered, we would not be tempted to lose heart!

Other passages also encourage us to be persistent in our prayers, such as the parable about the man who doesn't want to get up and answer his neighbor knocking at his door in the middle of the night, but finally opens it and gets food for his neighbor because he *kept on* knocking. "Persistence will make him get up and give his friend all he wants" (Luke 11:8). I emphasize this because, if you watch evangelists on TV and only learn about healing prayer from them, you may hear nothing (or, at best, very little) about the cost in time and energy you may have to expend to bring God's healing to a deeply wounded, hurting person.

We use the word "soaking" because it conveys an image of placing a sick person in a tub of water and surrounding him or her with warmth. It reminds me of the famous shrine dedicated to Our Lady at Lourdes in France, where much healing takes place. The sick are lowered into the chilly water that flows out of the mountain streams. At Lourdes the water is so cold that you don't relax when they lower you into the water. God often uses the cleansing stream to heal the sick (one of my friends was healed there). One of the amazing things is that when the pilgrims come out of the bracing bath, the water dries off immediately, and they don't seem to catch cold.

Relaxing in the Presence of God

When we pray using soaking prayer, we simply get a team together (or at home you can pray one-on-one if you like), and then we gather around and lay our hands on the sick person. We say a simple prayer, asking God to heal that person. We don't need to keep on repeating the prayer; we can just let the sick person relax in the presence of Jesus while the team simply remains quiet or prays quietly. Most people feel a need to say or do something; but the simple presence of Jesus, which we all bear within us, is often enough to bring healing. For those who would like to be active in prayer, they (or the group) can pray the

Rosary. Or those who are part of the Catholic Charismatic Renewal can pray in tongues. (The idea behind "praying in tongues" is that we turn our prayer over to the Holy Spirit, who knows best how to pray for the sick person.)

One of the wonderful things about soaking prayer is that everyone involved seems to sense God's presence and is spiritually refreshed. Also, you are free to decide how long to pray; it can be as short as five minutes or, on the other hand, the prayer can occasionally go on for days, with the team taking turns.

The most memorable example of prolonged soaking prayer in my own life happened in 1975 in Colombia, South America, when some members of our team came to me very excited after they had started praying for a young woman who had a disfigured leg that was at least six inches shorter than her normal leg. While they prayed, they thought that they were seeing the bent bone in her leg straightening, and so the team wanted me to see what was happening. I gladly joined them to pray and watch what was going on. It was a slow process, but it did seem to be happening—a miracle of bone growth and trans-formation. Slow or not, it was exciting.

This healing occurred during a priests' retreat. The local bishop, Bishop Uribe Jaramillo, was attending the retreat, and we invited him to join the team. By the end of that first day, everyone on the retreat had heard what was happening. The girl's name was Teresita, and her story was tragic but typical of the poor. When she was a child walking barefooted through a swamp, she cut her foot on something sharp in the water. Lacking the proper medical attention, the puncture wound had become infected and eventually reached the bone, where it developed into osteomyelitis, which drastically affected the growth of her bones, especially the tibia. She could walk but only with the aid of a crutch. A large group, including Bishop Uribe himself, pitched in and took turns praying, and it seemed clear that her bones were slowly straightening and lengthening.

Twice the healing process stopped, and someone on the team noticed that this happened whenever her mother came into the room. Talking to Teresita, the team discovered that she blamed her mother for not getting her the medical attention that she needed as a child. The mother, of course, was too poor to pay a physician and was not at fault. We asked Teresita to forgive her mother. In a moving scene, she prayed and asked for Jesus' help and was able to forgive her mother. Once again the leg started growing!

As you can see, we were all learning experientially about the gospel truth that if we are to be forgiven, we first need to forgive our enemies. Unless that happened, no healing could take place. That first day the soaking prayer took *hours*, but by the end of the day, there had been a notable visual change and Teresita's leg had grown perhaps two inches (out of the earlier six-inch discrepancy).

The next day prayers for Teresita went on all day long, and her leg seemed to grow another inch or so.

When I left Colombia to return to the United States, the Colombians themselves continued praying faithfully under Bishop Uribe's leadership. Later we learned that Teresita eventually was able to walk, with some difficulty but without a crutch. Bishop Uribe later became a leader (in the late 1970s) of the Charismatic Renewal in Latin America.

What happened was not just a healing in the normal course of nature but was a real supernatural event, beyond the ordinary, in which we saw bones straighten and grow. The crucial ingredient was the persistent prayer that Jesus encouraged when he told the story of the faithful widow who persuaded the reluctant judge who didn't seem to be listening.

Many times I have seen Jesus respond to soaking prayer when we place the patient in his loving presence. Just to take another example: In San Diego in 1978, our team prayed for three young people who were all suffering with scoliosis (curvature of the spine). Often the only way to treat scoliosis is through surgery. The entire group of three hundred people attending that retreat helped us pray, and in the course of two days, all three of those crooked spines notably shifted and straightened.

The gospel clearly encourages us to take time when we pray for the sick. Just take your time and keep on asking, and you may see remarkable results. Please try it, and see what happens!

FOUR

OTHER TYPES OF
HEALING

Even though we have experienced many extraordinary physical, bodily healings, the most extraordinary healings that I have witnessed were emotional and spiritual. In this chapter, we'll discuss inner healing from emotional wounds, as well as healing from sin, which is healing of our wills and spirits.

INNER (EMOTIONAL) HEALING

Almost every family we know is suffering from wounded relationships and the devastating effects of what people do to one another. To take a common example, counselors estimate that one out of four women and one out of five men have experienced sexual abuse. These traumatic experiences usually leave permanent wounds that deeply impair the victim's ability to relate normally to family members in the present. When our early memories are impaired by neglect or directly wounded by harshness, we tend to pass on this woundedness to our own family. What is not *transformed* through Christ's redeeming our pain through the cross is usually *transmitted* to the people we live with.

For me, one of the greatest things I have ever learned is the possibility that Jesus can, through his own suffering, change our weaknesses and even make them into strengths.

An entire book could be written on inner healing (and there are some excellent books on this topic). Although we don't have the space here to go into depth on this subject, I would like to share with you a simple method of praying that may change your life (and the lives of your friends) in a profound way.

Most important, unless we are trained in counseling, when we pray with each other for inner healing, we should not go beyond

- listening,
- loving,
- and praying with one another.

The great temptation is to give advice to other people. But we should refrain from doing so. If we have not received training as counselors or spiritual directors, we are not qualified to give advice, and we usually do more good by really listening in a loving way and then praying for blessing and healing. Simply praying can lead to extraordinary healing.

After I learned about praying for God's healing of people with deep emotional wounds, the very first person I prayed with received an extraordinary healing, which was very encouraging to me. The woman was a religious who had been in a mental hospital for years, consumed with extreme anger and bitterness. Her psychiatrist had asked me to visit her to encourage her and pray for her. Twice I had appointments with her, and she simply refused to talk to me. You can imagine how frustrating that is: to have an hour's appointment with someone who simply clams up and will not talk. It was a monologue with no response, and I'm not a particularly talkative person in any case. Eventually, the sister was released from the hospital—not cured but medicated enough so that she wouldn't hurt herself.

About this time I learned about inner healing ("healing of the memories") from a course given by a great teacher of inner healing, Agnes Sanford. A short time later, I was traveling through the city where the sister was assigned at her motherhouse, so I telephoned just as a courtesy to see how she was doing. She wanted to see me, and so I agreed to do so. When I arrived, I realized that she was still suffering from profound depression and anger. I also realized that psychiatry had done whatever was medically possible, and so I also knew that the last hope of her ever getting better was simply to pray for her healing. So I told her what I had learned about Jesus healing people of their inner wounds. I didn't particularly want to suggest praying with her because I had learned that you don't start by praying for the most difficult or impossible cases; instead, you start with something simple (and humanly speaking, her condition was impossible.)

Since there was no one else to help her, I decided to run the risk of failure. (Remember when I said that faith is spelled R-I-S-K?) So I told her what I had learned about inner healing and then asked if she would like me to pray in this way. I was half hoping she would say no. To my surprise, she said yes, which was the first positive response I had ever gotten from her in all our conversations.

So I was caught! I knew what the key circumstances were in her broken family relationships when she was growing up and what resentments had been growing that had resulted in her sullen anger. I really didn't have much human hope that anything would happen when I prayed. The problem was too huge, and any prayer that I might say was too simple. But prayer looked like it was her last chance, so I had to take it.

So I did what Agnes Sanford had suggested. I walked around and stood behind the chair in which she was sitting and put my hand on her shoulder. I closed my eyes so I wouldn't be distracted (or discouraged) by looking at her, and I simply asked Jesus to be present to us in a special way and to go back with her to all those times when she had been hurt by rejection as a child. At most, the prayer took five minutes. When I finished, I didn't want to open my eyes because I didn't have the confidence that anything had happened. But finally, I opened my eyes to look at her. To my surprise she was gently crying, which I recognized immediately as a breakthrough, because the only emotion she had ever shown before was anger. And here she was, showing her pain and sadness. Then it was time for her to leave.

A few weeks later, she wrote to say that something had really happened. The clouds, as it were, had parted, and the sun had finally broken through. And her life changed. Of course she still had some problems, but nothing like what she had been experiencing previously. Two years later, I met her when I was again passing through the city where she lived, and she was smiling—and it was the first time I had ever seen her smile.

That was the first time I witnessed Jesus healing someone in this way. Since then, I've seen it many times.

If someone opens up to you about their sorrows that are deeply affecting their life, here's how you can pray with them. You don't need to know much or be a professional counselor to pray in this way.

1. Choose a quiet place and arrange for it to remain quiet, free from phone calls for an hour or more.

2. Ideally you should have a prayer partner, especially if you are praying for someone of the opposite sex.

3. Say an opening prayer, asking for the guidance and protection of the Holy Spirit. If the person you are praying for can also pray, encourage him or her to do so. And ask Mary, the mother of Jesus, to intercede for you and help you.

4. Now you come to the heart of the prayer. Ask Jesus to come into the room, as it were, and take over. Remain in silence for a while and see what happens. Even if the

person you are praying for doesn't say anything, you usually will have a sense that something is (or isn't) going on.

I am always amazed at those times when the person we are praying for actually "sees" Jesus coming into the scene. When he appears, he is usually very strong—not wispy, as he is portrayed in so much religious art. He has the strong muscular arms of a carpenter, and he is very manly, but gentle and direct. Then he does the simple human things that the person needed at the time when the trauma occurred. I have been praying when he played baseball with a man who never had a chance to take part in athletics as a boy. He has taken someone into his strong arms like a brother when the person needed to cry. Jesus is infinitely creative, loving, and real.

At times he brings his mother, Mary, into the scene, especially when the person is missing a mother's love. At least four times, I've been there when Mary seems to have appeared to a Protestant, who was certainly not expecting it. There are so many different ways that Jesus heals people!

It should also be said that Jesus does not always appear to people when we pray. Some people are simply not very visual or imaginative. If nothing seems to happen when you pray with someone, you should not in any way make that person feel guilty. If the person you are praying with doesn't "see" Jesus, then you can pray and ask Jesus to guide your own prayer, and you can voice that prayer. However, it's important not to put any pressure on the person you are praying with to accept anything you say, especially if it doesn't seem right to him or her.

You will find that most people among your acquaintances probably need some inner healing. Not everything that happens to us is traumatic. Many times it's just something that was *missing* in our relationships that needs healing—for example, a father in the military who simply wasn't home very often. Friends who work in prison ministry tell me that almost everyone in jail suffers a missing-father wound. We are a nation, they say, of lost sons crying out for their missing fathers.

If you become deeply involved in the ministry of inner healing, learn all you can about it through reading books, attending conferences, and meeting with others who have taken up this marvelous work. Our situation is the same as that which disturbed Jesus, who saw that the people around him were harassed and dejected, like sheep without a shepherd (see Matthew 9:35-38). And the response of Jesus was one of compassion, which drove him to ask his Father to send more laborers into the vineyard. Do you realize that *you*, perhaps, are the answer to his prayer?

HEALING FROM SIN

When we talk about healing prayer, our thoughts usually go to physical healing, the healing of our bodies, but we also realize that our forgiveness and healing from *sin* is the most important healing of all. As Catholics, we are familiar with the Sacrament of Reconciliation, which is meant to deliver us from the guilt of sin.

As you know, when we repent of sin, we are mostly dealing with the past. Basically, we confess to God that we knowingly and willingly did something sinful. We tell God that we're sorry, and we promise to make amends for the past and firmly resolve to do the right thing in the future—to "sin no more" (John 8:11).

In his ministry, the great evangelist Billy Graham also dealt with sin in this way, trying to awaken repentance in his listeners by portraying with vivid descriptions the devastation that sin wreaks in our lives. As we know, Graham's preaching met with great success in helping people to repent and change their lives. And again, his preaching concentrated on repenting for the past and making a resolution to change in the future.

But what I would like to discuss is the *present*. Our fallen human condition, which is always with us, sets us up for sin and takes away some of our freedom. It's that weakness—our "predominant fault"—that leads us to go on committing the same sins over and over again. Jesus addressed this inner weakness when he taught us the Our Father and said, "Lead us not into temptation but deliver us from evil" (Matthew 6:13, RSV) or, as the New Jerusalem translation puts it, "Do not put us to the test, but save us from the Evil One."

In his Letter to the Romans, St. Paul speaks for us when he shares his disgust with our fallen human condition and cries out in agony about how he has failed to live up to his high ideals. Instead, he does the very things he hates:

> I have been sold as a slave to sin. I cannot understand my own behavior. I fail to carry out the things I want to do, and I find myself doing the very things I hate. . . . When I act against my own will, then, it is not my true self doing it, but sin which lives in me. (Romans 7:14-16, 20 JB)

As you can see, Paul is talking about sin in a way that doesn't concentrate on specific actions that we know are wrong but we willingly do anyway; he is talking about the sin that underlies the sinful actions, the hidden foundations of sins. They are not just the sins that we willingly commit, but the sin "which lives in me" (Romans 7:20).

This is the very deep reservoir of sin that lives in all of us, which I want to address because we have discovered that the Holy Spirit can really do something about those dark forces that we find within ourselves. In fact, at the end of this passage in Romans, Paul cries out in agony: "Who will rescue me from this body doomed to death?" (Romans 7:24), and then he answers his own desperate cry: "God—thanks be to him—through Jesus Christ our Lord" (7:25).

And so, here we are, not only talking about asking God's forgiveness for our past sins, but for help in overcoming a permanent evil condition from which God is able to rescue us through his healing power.

How can we be healed of the evil tendencies that drive us to repeat the same sin over and over again and that, over time, can lead to addictions? Personally, I have read very little about this crucial area of our Christian faith journey. We need to be aware of how sin gains a foothold in our lives. So I want to share with you what we've learned.

Sinful Habits

We all know that if we repeatedly sin in some area of our lives, we build up a hardness in our hearts that makes it easier to repeat the sin and that can desensitize us until we come to accept and no longer abhor the sin. A good example in our culture is pornography, to which many men—and some women too—are addicted. No longer do addicts need to go outside their homes to see seductive movies; they can simply click their way to porn using their computers. And sadly enough, a sizeable number of clergy—both Catholic and Protestant—are addicted.

Any sin, repeated over time, creates a habitual pattern that makes it easier to sin. One time I recognized that danger in my own life. I was on the road some years ago, staying in a hotel. Aware of the danger of becoming addicted to pornography, I have always tried to avoid it, but that afternoon I was just trying to relax, and so I turned on the TV. The program that came on piqued my curiosity—that was my weakness in this incident. The image was of a man and woman, both very attractive and semi-clad in black. I was very curious: What were they doing? As I watched, I found myself mysteriously attracted to the screen. As I mentioned, curiosity was the trap. After a minute or so, I recognized that the attraction in me was somehow evil and had a power in it greater than ordinary. Fortunately, I recognized the danger and realized that if I continued to gaze at the TV image, I would in some way become hooked.

In one sense this is no big deal; this kind of thing happens all the time. But if we give in to little things, it can lead to sin gradually becoming entrenched in our hearts and minds. The example above is very simple, but it is significant because this is the way harmful habits are usually established. When we notice in our own lives that something has happened that might harm us, we need to quickly pray and ask God to free us from anything dangerous that might attach itself to us. You can say a short heartfelt prayer like this one:

O Lord, you know what just happened to me and what thoughts went through my mind. Please take away anything evil that might have been part of those thoughts and desires. By the power of your

Holy Spirit, please fill my mind with your thoughts and desires so that I can become more and more like you.

Addictions

Habitual sinful actions and thoughts that are indulged in over a period of time can gradually be strengthened until they reach the level of an addiction, which draws us into sin and takes away some of our freedom. The good news of the gospel is that Jesus Christ can truly break the power of addiction—sometimes with a one-time prayer and at other times with persistent prayer. Among the addictions that come to mind is alcoholism. Another is smoking, the habit that affects so many aspects of our physical health.

All these addictions can be the subject of our prayer. For example, even though she had been a missionary in Israel for the Southern Baptists, my wife, Judith, was addicted to cigarettes. One of her colleagues was concerned enough to pray for her for three days. He said, "Every time you feel like smoking, let me know, and I will pray with you." She gave him permission to do so—but not wholeheartedly. After three days she drove him to the airport and, after seeing him off, immediately lit up a cigarette in the airport lobby. To her surprise it tasted terrible, so she put it out. That was more than thirty years ago, and she hasn't smoked since!

One of the more powerful examples of healing from a life-threatening addiction occurred when I was in St. Louis, stationed at Merton House, a small prayer center. Some friends asked if I would be willing to pray with a woman who was drinking herself to death. She was about sixty years old and had been given the very best professional treatment, at great expense to her family. She had spent some time in a residential treatment center (and we are aware of the great work that is accomplished through such treatment), but nothing had helped her. In fact, she was worse, because when she was trying to quit, her mood became so dark and her actions so hurtful that her whole family was miserable and decided that they would have peace in their home only if they let her drink whenever she wanted.

I agreed to pray with her, and one morning the woman's friends drove her to Merton House (she took a couple of stiff drinks to summon up the courage to go). When she arrived with her friends, my prayer was very simple: I just asked Jesus to take away her need to drink. The effect was immediate (it usually doesn't happen this quickly): She simply stopped drinking.

And it wasn't only that she stopped and that her will was strengthened; the very desire to drink was taken from her and the very "occasions of sin" were no longer problems for her. For example, she was able to go to the store and walk past the bottles of wine on the shelves and not even experience the temptation to drink (which had been so overwhelming previously). It is just amazing how often Jesus helps people become free of destructive habits and addictions.

The basic prayer to end an addiction is very simple: You ask Jesus to break it. In becoming free of an addiction, God may give us the strength of will to say no when the temptation comes, or we simply are freed from even the desire to give in to the temptation. To clarify, the following outcomes are possible:

1. Sometimes the addiction is amazingly remedied by prayer, and the person is totally freed.

2. More often the prayer helps, but the addict also has to take all the human steps that are necessary. Most alcoholics, for example, need to join Alcoholics Anonymous and attend the meetings. If they are financially able, they can go to a treatment center. Usually we are not preserved from taking all the remedies that everyone else needs to take. The healing comes from a combination of treatment and prayer. It's not an "either-or" situation but a "both-and" one.

3. Sometimes the addict continues to struggle with the addiction, and the prayer seems to have no discernible effect. (This has been true of several dear friends.)

Our advice is to take every possible means of helping the person. There is much mystery in all of this. As I mentioned earlier, for six years we prayed for our daughter, Rachel, for her asthma. Then one night through the prayer of two friends, she was instantly healed. Jesus recommends that we need to "pray continually and never lose heart" (Luke 18:1).

Occasionally, a dramatic and instant healing of addiction (and also of physical diseases like cancer) takes place. However, we should have expectant faith that, regardless of how it happens, great good comes out of our prayers. I have seen so many wonderful things take place that I believe it is a sad mistake not to pray whenever we have the chance. We have everything to gain, with little to lose.

Praying for Freedom and the Power to Forgive

As Catholics, we can learn to pray for Jesus to *free* us from our addictions and sinful habits. It is especially helpful to learn to pray for these weaknesses in the intimacy of our families. For example, if a married person is struggling with a drinking problem, the natural place to pray is with someone in the immediate family.

The problem of addiction, in particular, embarrasses many Christians, not only because it drives them to commit habitual sins, but also because it becomes difficult, if not impossible, for them to live up to their ideals. What we have found in our experience is that healing and freeing prayer is a key to winning this struggle to live up to our Christian values.

Here is one unusual example: I heard Reverend Dennis Bennett, the first Anglican priest to be baptized in the Spirit (in 1959), describe how he used to experience lustful temptations in his dreams (of course, we are not responsible for our desires when we are asleep). But after his baptism in the Spirit, even his dreams were freed from those lustful thoughts and temptations.

The practice of going to confession has declined considerably in recent years, but I think that if priests would learn to say prayers after the sacramental confession asking Jesus to heal the sinful tendencies and addictions attached to the sins that have been confessed, people would flock to confession. I think a sensitive confessor who prays for people in a realistic way might even become occupied full-time in praying for God's hurting people.

The most prominent obstacles to our receiving healing are hatred and unforgiveness. If we do not forgive others for what they have done to hurt us, we, in turn, will not receive forgiveness for our sins. "Yes, if you forgive others their failings, your heavenly Father will forgive you yours; but if you do not forgive others, your Father will not forgive your failings either" (Matthew 6:14-15).

Forgiving our enemies is difficult and sometimes humanly impossible, and so we need to ask Jesus to give us a share of his own forgiving love. This will enable us to love others with God's own love for his people. "The love of God has been poured into our hearts by the Holy Spirit which has been given to us" (Romans 5:5). Your prayer—with your spouse, spiritual director, or prayer partner—can go something like this:

> Lord Jesus Christ, send your Holy Spirit into my life and fill me with your love for people. Especially in regard to _____ [Name], whom I have a hard time forgiving, help me to see him [or her] as you see him. Take out of my heart the desire to get even. Show me some good quality in him that I haven't seen before. I pray that you bless this person in abundance. Free me from any judgmentalism on my part, and help me to love the person as you do. If he needs to change, help him do that, but help me to change too, and show me any areas where I may be blind. Pour out your love into my heart. Forgive me my sins as I forgive those who have hurt me.
>
> Give me the power through your Spirit for my hidden self to grow strong, so that Christ may live in my heart through faith. And then, planted in love and built on love, I will have strength to grasp the breadth and the length, the height and the depth until, knowing the love of Christ, I am filled with the utter fullness of God. (The last part of this prayer is based on Ephesians 3:16-19.)

As we know, the greatest commandment of Jesus is to love as he loved, and we need his help in prayer to receive this greatest gift of all!

FIVE

The Medical Connection

As Catholics, we are proud that historically the first hospitals were established under the Church's inspiration by our ancestors, who took seriously Jesus' command to care for the sick. In chapter 25 of the Gospel of Matthew, Jesus says he will separate the sheep (the saved) from the goats (the lost) based, among other things, on whether we visit and care for the sick. If we try to relieve their pain, we will be rewarded "when the Son of man comes in his glory" (25:31). Then our Lord will say to us, "In so far as you did this to one of the least of these brothers of mine, you did it to me" (25:40).

We rejoice that the Red Cross was initially inspired by St. Camillus de Lellis (1550–1614), a gambler whose conversion led him to dedicate his life to caring for the sick. Eventually, Camillus gathered followers and founded a new religious congregation in Rome whose members cared for the sick, including plague victims and those wounded in battle.

In recent times we have witnessed the work of Blessed Mother Teresa of Calcutta, who continued the Church's long tradition of caring for the sick and dying through the religious order she founded, the Missionaries of Charity. In 1979 she won the Nobel Peace Prize for her work. While she was alive, if you asked, "Who is a saint today?" most people—Protestant as well as Catholic, non-Christian as well as Christian—would probably have answered, "Mother Teresa!"

So from the very beginnings of Christianity, one of the great works of our Church has been to take care of the sick. In the early years of Christianity, "caring for the sick was a *unique* contribution of Christianity. The pagans did not care for their sick in any organized" way.[10]

Our Christian values and the example of so many saints inspire many Catholic medical professionals to give their lives to healing the sick in our society. Because of our history, Catholics are not likely to downplay the practice of medicine.

Unfortunately, some fervent Christians set up an opposition between science and religion. Their thinking goes like this: "If you have faith, all you need to do is pray that God will heal you. In fact, taking medicine is a sign that you don't have faith. If you are a real Christian, you will throw away your pills." In their understanding, if you do take medicine, you have chosen a lower path that shows that you really don't have a strong faith. I hope you have never encountered this attitude, but it has led many sick people into great anguish as they wonder what to do.

Fortunately, Catholics usually don't have to deal with this painful inner conflict. Catholics do not view medical treatment as being in competition with healing prayer. We have a "both-and" attitude: both prayer and medicine, not one or the other.

In the Book of Sirach, we find a powerful chapter that says that sometimes God heals us through a physician's care or through medicine, but that at other times,

God heals us directly through prayer. Unfortunately, in the Protestant Bible, Sirach (also titled Ecclesiasticus) is included only in the Apocrypha, but for Catholics it is considered among the inspired texts. Here's what Sirach has to say about turning to prayer, to physicians, and to pharmacists for help when we are sick:

> Treat the doctor with the honour that is his due,
>> in consideration of his services;
>>> for he too has been created by the Lord.
> Healing itself comes from the Most High,
>> like a gift received from a king.
> The doctor's learning keeps his head high,
>> and the great regard him with awe.
> The Lord has brought forth medicinal herbs from
>> the ground,
>> and no one sensible will despise them.
> Did not a piece of wood once sweeten the water,
>> thus giving proof of its power?
> He has also given some people knowledge,
>> so that they may draw credit from his mighty
>> works.
> He uses these for healing and relieving pain;
>> the druggist makes up a mixture from them.
> Thus, there is no end to his activities;
>> thanks to him, well-being exists throughout the
>> world.

My child, when you are ill, do not rebel,
　　but pray to the Lord and he will heal you.
Renounce your faults, keep your hands unsoiled,
　　and cleanse your heart from all sin.
Offer incense and a memorial of fine flour,
　　make as rich an offering as you can afford.
Then let the doctor take over—the Lord created
　　　him too—
　　do not let him leave you, for you need him.
There are times when good health depends on
　　　doctors.
For they, in their turn, will pray the Lord
　　to grant them the grace to relieve
　　and to heal, and so prolong your life.
Whoever sins in the eyes of his Maker,
　　let such a one come under the care of the doctor!
　　(Sirach 38:1-15)

This is an amazing passage, considering that it was written several hundred years before the birth of Christ, at a time when physicians and pharmacists were just a step removed from witch doctors and herbalists. It clearly states that there are times when prayer has the advantage in leading us to healing but that there are other times when we need doctors (because they too pray that God will use their skills). At other times God will use the drugs that the pharmacist prepares to make us well. This scriptural passage helps us to see that we can combine prayer with the best that modern science has to offer. God can work through any or all of it.

Recently, my sister was diagnosed with breast cancer, and we are praying for her healing. In the meantime, the surgeons have performed a lumpectomy, and she is also undergoing radiation treatments. And so, like the author of Sirach, we believe that combining healing prayer, medicine, and the physicians' treatments is all part of a wise God's care for the sick.

MEDICINE AND HEALING PRAYER

Over the years, we have learned many wonderful ways to help along the healing process. One friend who is a nurse prays when she comes to work, asking God to bless all the medications she will distribute that day in the hospital. In her prayer, she asks God to use the medications to achieve the healing purpose the physicians had in mind when they prescribed them. In addition, she prays that God will block any negative or harmful side effects. From her example, we can learn to pray against the injurious side effects of chemo or any other treatments. For example, if you—or a friend—is undergoing treatment for cancer, you can pray to prevent the loss of hair, energy, or appetite. For years now we have done this, and we have heard many wonderful testimonies of how God has maintained a patient's life and energy. In some cases, the predicted hair loss simply didn't happen!

As we can see, there are several basic purposes in our praying:

1. To bring healing directly to the sick person;

2. To increase the healing brought about through drugs or medicine; and

3. To block any harmful side effects of the treatment.

You can pray this way at home even for something as commonplace as a cold. Of course, the stakes are very high when cancer strikes, and then it becomes even more important for us to pray. You can create your own prayer to support the efforts of your physician. And when you pray for a cancer patient, you can ask God to make the cancer disappear. This really does happen often, and when it does, you will have reason to rejoice!

Just to give you an idea of how you might compose a prayer over your medication or treatment, here is a model you can use:

Lord Jesus, I come before you with this medication, and I ask you to bless it and use it for healing in the way the doctor intends. Increase its healing properties, and let it bless and benefit my body. And by the power of your Holy Spirit, block every possible harmful side effect. [Here mention what these might be.] Please fill me with your life and with your health.

I thank you now and forever for your great love for me and my family. We love you now and forever. And Mary, our Mother, please pray for us, now and at the hour of our death. Amen.

The most important thing is to *pray*, *pray*, *pray* and to believe that our God is on the side of *life*!

THE MEDICAL EVIDENCE

Most physicians are not impressed by the testimonies of individual healings that they see on television programs sponsored by healing evangelists. They think that prayer groups are far too casual in talking about "miracles." Many Catholics have heard about the Medical Bureau in Lourdes, France, which reviews thousands of reported healings among the pilgrims but authenticates only about one every two to three years as being beyond the possibility of a human, scientific explanation. We certainly can appreciate their position of asking for credible scientific proof that God really does answer our prayers.

The Church has always been reluctant to claim that a *miracle* of healing has taken place. In 1974 I had the wonderful opportunity to spend three days at the famous shrine in Lourdes and spoke at length with the physician who was in charge of the Medical Bureau. He told me how frustrating it was to see so many remarkable healings taking place without being able to authenticate them because it is so difficult to meet the six stringent conditions that have to be present for a healing to be declared as scientifically verified.

For example, one of the conditions is that the patient can't be taking any medication that could have possibly caused the cure. But what cancer patient under a doctor's care is not receiving radiation or some other medical treatment? As a result, the doctors have examined thousands of patients in whom measurable physical changes have taken place that they could not verify as a miraculous cure. Most ordinary observers could see that God had healed numerous patients, but nevertheless, the rigorous conditions could not be met to deem it a miracle.

In World War II, I served as a medic in a United States Army hospital (Camp Crowder, Missouri), and so, when I later discovered healing prayer, I had a strong desire to offer some credible evidence to the medical community. With this hope in mind, our staff at Christian Healing Ministries worked with the physician Dale Matthews and planned a study to help determine whether healing prayer produces actual physical healing that could be scientifically verified. We chose to study rheumatoid arthritis because it is a disease that is at present incurable.

In 1996 we prayed for patients who were receiving treatment from a pain and arthritis clinic in Clearwater,

Florida, directed by a nurse practitioner, Sally Marlowe. The patients were volunteers, and not all were Christian. We formed a dozen teams that prayed with the arthritic patients for three days. The results were truly extraordinary, and the study was later published in the *Southern Medical Journal*.[11]

Some forty patients in two groups were studied. To qualify, each patient had to have at least six swollen joints and nine tender joints. The patients were assessed using ten different tests, and there was a twelve-month follow-up. Our study did not use the double-blind approach that scientists prefer; it was face-to-face. We gave six separate teachings (on topics such as forgiveness) and prayed as we usually do, talking to the patients and praying with the laying on of hands. This, of course, meant that some measure of the placebo effect could not be ruled out.

The effects of prayer seemed truly marvelous in at least four categories: (1) the average number of *tender* joints at the beginning of the study was 16.8, and at the end of twelve months it was only 5.7; (2) the number of *swollen* joints at the beginning was 9.8, but at the end was 3.1; (3) the number of *painful* joints was 4.5 at the beginning and 3.1 at the end; and (4) the *grip* strength also was improved. These changes were all statistically significant.

It appeared that four of the patients were totally healed, and most showed some physical improvement.

Dr. Matthews stated that the physical results could not be explained by chance and that the introduction of prayer into the treatment had the same effect as a *new drug*. (The patients were already taking medications such as steroids.) A significant finding was that the patients' improvement did not diminish during the following year. If we had been trying a new drug, the benefits would have peaked during treatment and then disappeared over the course of time. Instead, the patients maintained the degree of healing they had experienced initially.

The beautiful thing was that when we prayed for the physical healing of the patients, we saw not only physical changes but a transformation of their attitudes as they experienced how much God loves them! For many, the God who had seemed distant now felt much more real, and those who were weighed down with sorrow were now lifted up with joy.[12]

From our point of view, the conditions of prayer were not the best; for example, as stated, the patients were not all Christian. One even said, "You pray to your God, and I'll pray to mine!"

You may never engage in a scientific study of prayer but now, more than ever before, we see the scientific and medical community becoming aware of a real possibility of healing taking place when people pray. What was once unheard of is now becoming commonplace. We just never were encouraged to pray with the sick—especially with the laying on of hands. But something remarkable is happening when a physician, Dr. Larry Dossey, has the audacity to write that he looks forward to a day when doctors can be sued for malpractice if they don't pray for their sick patients, because scientific studies now demonstrate that prayer really benefits health![13]

SIX

THE HEALING EFFECTS
OF THE SACRAMENTS AND
SACRAMENTALS

The sacraments confer grace because Christ is at work in them (see *Catechism of the Catholic Church*, 1127). So of course we would expect the grace of healing in a sacramental setting, especially the Sacrament of the Sick, but also in the Sacraments of Reconciliation, the Eucharist, and Baptism. In this chapter, I'll address the healing aspects of the sacraments and the exciting ways the Church in recent years is rediscovering the marvelous healing power of the sacramental life. In addition, I'll also talk about how sacramentals—usually blessed oil, water, and salt—can be used effectively in healing prayer.

ANOINTING OF THE SICK

Today the Sacrament of the Anointing of the Sick is once more being used as a means of bringing healing to our bodies and souls. Before the Second Vatican Council (1962–1965), the Anointing of the Sick was called "Extreme Unction," meaning it was the Last Anointing. The sacrament's purpose was primarily to prepare the sick person for a holy death. If you talk to people who remember those days, they will tell you that the families of sick people often dreaded seeing the priest coming into the hospital room with his vestments, candles, and oils (chrisms). It meant that the sick person was *in extremis*—in other words, "in danger of death"—which was at that time the necessary condition for receiving Extreme

Unction. "Am I that bad off?" was the natural reaction of the sick patient.

Remarkably, a few patients were healed in those days, and some older priests can tell you extraordinary stories about patients who had been given up for dead but who were amazingly restored to health after receiving Extreme Unction. But such a cure was rare and was certainly not expected.

But now, after the Second Vatican Council, the Church has returned to its ancient belief in the Anointing of the Sick as a sacrament that can bring healing on every level—spiritual and emotional as well as physical (see *Catechism of the Catholic Church*, 1499–1513). No longer does the patient need to be in danger of death but simply must have a serious condition worthy of prayer. The "oil of the sick" is traditionally consecrated by the bishop during Holy Week, and when he prays over the oil, he asks God to "make this oil a remedy for all who are anointed with it; heal them in body, in soul, and in spirit, and deliver them from every affliction." Not only does the sacrament prepare a person for death, but now it is also intended to bring healing to the body. Both purposes are part of the sacrament.

In the early centuries of the Church's life, it was common for people to take home blessed oil and use it for anointing whenever the oil was needed for healing. Baptized Catholics—laypeople—kept it in the ancient equivalent of the medicine cabinet.

As centuries went by, the Sacrament of Penance became connected with receiving the anointing, to make sure that the recipient was free of sin before receiving a sacrament in a worthy manner. However, in the Middle Ages, the penances became so severe that most people would normally only receive penance once in a lifetime. They would put off receiving anointing until the end of their lives, so from the ninth century until the Second Vatican Council, the sacrament was connected almost exclusively with preparing to die worthily. This meant that bodily healing was not expected, and because the anointing was a sacrament, only priests were allowed to minister it. And since a last confession was now connected with the anointing, it became a private ceremony, rather than one in which family and friends gathered around to pray together.

But now, once again, the reformed, renewed ceremony encourages the entire family and community to take part. As we realize, this represents an enormous change. The anointing is meant to be preceded normally by friends and relatives visiting the sick, at which time they can say their own prayers for blessing and healing.

This is the prayer the priest says while anointing the patient's forehead: "Through this holy anointing, may the Lord in his love and mercy help you with the grace of the Holy Spirit." The priest then anoints the sick person's hands while saying, "May the Lord who frees you from sin save you and raise you up." The "raise you up," of course, can mean a physical healing for some or a spiritual lifting for others.[14]

One of the other exciting developments is that substance addictions or mental or emotional illness is now considered sufficient reason to seek sacramental anointing.

Many parishes and hospital chapels now offer regular anointing services, and patients have plenty of opportunities to receive the Anointing of the Sick, which was not possible just a few short years ago. We are now encouraged to make the fullest use of these opportunities to receive healing prayer.

HEALING IN THE EUCHARIST

Since the Lord is especially present during the Mass, the celebration of the Eucharist is an especially suitable setting for God to heal the sick. For Catholics it seems natural for a priest to offer the votive Mass for healing of the sick and then to pray individually (when possible) for people, who can come forward to the altar. Fr. Ed McDonough, CSSR, used to walk through the church sprinkling people with holy water, and because of his special gifts, many people in the pews would feel God's healing power flow through them.

I will never forget the first time I actually saw healing take place through the Eucharist. A friend had just received Communion in his hand, and he was on his way to drink from the chalice when suddenly he was so overcome with God's presence that he had to sit down. So he sat for about a minute and then went on to drink the Precious Blood. Afterward he told us that he had received such a powerful healing at that very time that he had to sit down and rest.

Since Catholics esteem the Mass so highly, I think there is a tendency for us to place too much emphasis on a healing Mass as our only way of holding a healing service. Although, as I have said, amazing healings do take place at Mass, there are several reasons that it should not be seen as the only channel for Catholics to receive healing.

In the first place, a full celebration of Mass usually takes nearly an hour, which means that there is less time for any individual ministry. Also, to hold a healing Mass means that a priest-celebrant is required who is familiar with how to celebrate such a Mass. Because many priests are not familiar with this type of celebration, many sick people may not have a chance to attend a healing Mass when they need one. Moreover, if the only opportunity that laypeople have of actually receiving healing prayer is during Mass, they may get the idea that priests are the only ones who are suited to praying effectively for the sick. At this time in history, it is especially important for laypeople to gain the confidence that they too, at home or at work, can pray for healing. In fact, the Lord may have given some of them a special gift of healing, and they need to be encouraged to start using that gift.

Inner Healing during Mass

The Eucharistic celebration is also a time when you can ask Jesus to heal you emotionally of past hurts. A friend of mine discovered a marvelous way to do this. She divided up her life into natural segments, and then at Mass she asked Jesus to heal her of anything that had wounded her during those time periods.

Of course, this is something we can all do. You simply break down your life into several natural divisions of time, such as year by year or by childhood, adolescence, young adulthood, and so forth. If you know, for example, that some key wounding took place when you were seven years old, you can start with that time period. At home, before Mass, spend some time writing down the blessings that you remember during that year, and then in another column, write down the painful things that wounded you, especially if they were connected with broken relationships, such as with your parents or authority figures like teachers.

When you are at Mass, make your special intention first of all a thanksgiving for all the good things that happened during that year. It's as if you are laying that list of blessings on the altar as a special thanksgiving. Then take the harmful things that you listed, and ask the Lord, especially as you receive him in Communion, to bring inner healing to each one. If you still bear ill will toward those who hurt you, you need to extend your forgiveness to them, with Jesus within you helping you do so.

Since this takes time, you can spend more time after Mass, either in the church or at home in God's special presence, giving thanks for all your blessings but also receiving healing and forgiveness for the wounds that you may have inflicted on others.

THE SACRAMENT OF RECONCILIATION

As we all realize, the number of Catholics going to confession has gone way down in recent years. And yet my experience has been that when people come to the priest for inner healing, they also demonstrate a deep desire to unburden their hearts by getting their sins out in the open and confessing them as best they can. I believe that the Sacrament of Reconciliation meets a very deep human need.

Unfortunately, many penitents have grown used to following a kind of stereotyped list—"I missed my morning prayers," etc.—instead of beginning with the spiritual problems that really weigh them down. People need to get away from such an approach and discuss what's really bothering them. The sins that Jesus preached against touch almost every one of us. Do we really love each other? When we have been hurt in a relationship, are we able to forgive? How do we relate to the members of our families and our colleagues at work?

Once we have shared our sins honestly with Jesus, who is represented by the priest, the priest can take the opportunity not only to forgive our sins but also to say a special prayer for us, the penitents, to be given the help that goes beyond our own willpower and to actually remove some of the weaknesses that lead to sin. This is not just a pious thought. I have seen countless penitents changed by Jesus so that their tendency to sin is weakened or even taken away. As we have mentioned, St. Paul admitted that he knew how he should act, but he just couldn't act virtuously: "I do the very things I hate," he confessed (Romans 7:15). And then he cried out to Jesus for help.

For some, I know this may sound too simple to be true, and I also know that not everyone that we pray for is instantly and totally healed, but it happens so often that it makes sense to pray after confession to help penitents be free of whatever it is that draws them into sin.

In addition, and this is not often discussed, there are evil spirits (of hatred and lust, for example) that may attach themselves to people who have made a habit of sinning. Pornography is a common, destructive sin that affects people and destroys marriage relationships. If priests learned to pray for God to take away those destructive habits, I believe enormous changes would take place in Catholic marriages.

I also believe that if a priest truly believed and compassionately practiced inner healing prayer in confession, the word would soon get around, and he could very well end up with a full-time ministry just hearing confessions.

Truly Jesus has the power to break the power of sin. It's not just that we can be freed of the guilt of sin, but we can also be freed of much of the attractive force of evil. Once I was speaking in Costa Rica to a group of about sixty college students. As I was speaking through an interpreter, suddenly, with no explanation, many students fell to the ground weeping. When I asked the interpreter what was going on, he told me that a powerful grace of repentance had just fallen upon the entire group, and their hearts had been touched in an extraordinary way.

THE SACRAMENT OF BAPTISM

Another channel of healing, which is not often recognized, is baptism. Mrs. Agnes Sanford, the wife of an Episcopal minister, shared many stories of how apparently dead babies came back to life when they were baptized. Her husband was often called upon to baptize "dying" babies, and "not one of them died."[15] This should not surprise us, since we believe that baptism brings us a *new birth* into the family of God. Baptism is a sacrament of life.

A surprising healing took place in 1968 when I baptized Suzie, the daughter of two friends in St. Louis. The mother asked me when I arrived whether she should take off the baby's diaper before we immersed her in the water in the baptismal font. I told her to take off the diaper, but the mother was hesitant because Suzie had been suffering from a very severe diaper rash since birth. She did take off the diaper, and I baptized Suzie. The next morning the rash had totally disappeared.

HEALING SACRAMENTALS

All Catholics are familiar with "sacramentals," especially the holy water with which we bless ourselves as we enter or leave a church. What we may not be aware of is the real healing power that can accompany our use of sacramentals.

I first learned about the amazing value of these sacramentals many years ago through the late Fr. Rick Thomas, SJ, who became famous for his work among the poor in El Paso, Texas. There on the Mexican border, Fr. Rick had developed a very simple—and extraordinary—ministry, which was based largely on his lively faith in the power of sacramentals.

For example, when a woman would come to Fr. Rick and tell him that her husband was unfaithful, he would bless a bottle of water and suggest that she use it to brew his coffee in the morning. Or he would bless a little bottle of salt and tell her to use it to season her husband's food for dinner. And he ordinarily used blessed oil when he prayed for and anointed a sick person. Fr. Rick discovered that these inexpensive remedies seemed to work and helped to increase the effectiveness of his healing prayers. Unusual as it might seem to actually drink holy water and not just make the "sign of the cross" with it, Fr. Rick said that drinking holy water was surprisingly effective and could cause a real change in those who consumed it.

The idea behind the sacramentals is that the common, ordinary elements that we use in our everyday lives can be blessed with a prayer in which a priest asks God to further endow them with his healing power to increase the natural curative powers they already possess. In the same way, we can pray over any medications we take, asking Jesus to increase the good effects that the doctors intended and prevent any harmful side effects.

Because God is invisible, we are helped when we offer him material elements that we can see and ask him to use them as channels of healing. In the course of Christian history, we find many materials that have been used, but the most important are

- *oil*—through anointing;
- w*ater*—through sprinkling or drinking; and
- *salt*—through sprinkling it in places or placing it on food.

Fortunately, all of these material elements are common and cost next to nothing.

We find remarkable stories in Scripture of God using these ordinary elements as special channels for his healing. Sometimes God chose very unusual materials for healing. For example, when the Israelites were bitten by serpents during their journey through the desert, some died, and God came up with an astonishing solution by ordering Moses to

> "make a fiery serpent and raise it as a standard. Anyone who is bitten and looks at it will survive." Moses then made a serpent out of bronze and raised it as a standard, and anyone who was bitten by a serpent and looked at the bronze serpent survived. (Numbers 21:8-9)

Later, when the Israelites began to worship the bronze serpent, God ordered it to be destroyed (see 2 Kings 18:4) because it had become idolatrous.

In the first three centuries of Christianity, laypeople, not just priests, used nonsacramental blessed oil to anoint the sick when they prayed for their healing. For example, the sixth century bishop St. Caesarius of Arles encouraged laypeople to take home blessed oil to anoint themselves and their families. In his history of the desert fathers, Palladius describes how the monk Macarius cured a paralyzed woman by anointing her and praying over her continuously for twenty days.[16]

For us, olive oil is mainly seen as a food, but in Jesus' time, it was also used to heal wounds. When the Good Samaritan took care of the man beaten by robbers, he "bandaged his wounds, pouring oil and wine on them" (Luke 10:34). (Wine, of course, with its alcohol content, was a first-century antiseptic.) In addition, oil has long been used as a symbol of the anointing of the Holy Spirit and of healing. "So they set off to proclaim repentance; and they cast out many devils, and anointed many sick people with oil and cured them" (Mark 6:12-13). However, a common concern among Church authorities is that people will confuse the special oil blessed for the Sacrament of the Anointing of the Sick with ordinary, unblessed oil that *anyone* can use. So naturally, they want to avoid any possible confusion by commissioning only priests and bishops to anoint with oil.

Holy water seems to magnify the power of the spoken prayer. I am convinced that there is a positive power imparted to the holy water so that when holy water accompanies the prayer, the spoken prayer for healing is more effective. What's fascinating is that when I have sprinkled a sick person with holy water, if there has been a demonic influence in that person's life, then there is often a real physical response to it. For example, when their foreheads were moistened, such people may react as if they have been burned—and yet the water is at room temperature. You can test the power of the blessing by then anointing the person with *unblessed* water; usually there is no reaction whatsoever!

Blessed salt has the advantage over water in that it doesn't evaporate but can stay in a room or place where it is sprinkled. It makes good sense to pray for places—such as hospital rooms—and then sprinkle a little salt around.

Through the sacraments, we are offered Jesus' life, and his life heals us, whether we need healing that is physical, spiritual, or emotional. The grace that is offered in the sacraments is available to us all. We should always turn to the gift of the sacraments, as well as to sacramentals, whenever we or our loved ones need healing.

Conclusion

I hope we have shown in these pages—from every perspective—that recovering our nearly lost heritage of healing prayer is an essential priority for our Church. If we believe that healing prayer actually heals the sick, our compassion will draw us to pray in imitation of our Lord. His compassion drew him to spend three years of public ministry in healing the sick.

In the beginning of this book, I mentioned that healing prayer gradually dwindled over the centuries until most of us never thought we could do it. But when we examine Sacred Scripture, Catholic tradition, and our human experience of witnessing that the sick are gloriously healed when we pray, we can be hopeful that the practice of healing prayer will be restored. That was my goal in writing this book.

If you have never tried to pray for someone's healing, I hope that you are now ready to consider starting— perhaps at home in a safe environment. If everyone who read this book were to pray for the healing of one sick family member or friend, then it would have accomplished its purpose. But that's only a start. I am confident that if you do begin praying for healing, it will change your life as well as deepen your relationship with God.

I also mentioned in the beginning that most Catholics—an overwhelming number—cannot remember their mothers or fathers ever praying *with* them when they were sick as children. I hope that fifty years from now, if someone were to ask a similar question, an overwhelming number would respond with a resounding yes!

If that should happen, it will mean that a wonderful, gentle revolution has taken place. There is no logical, coherent, biblical, or intellectual reason why it shouldn't happen. And so I end with this prayer:

Lord Jesus, I ask that you awaken within your Church a lively faith that you will come to our assistance when we are sick—spiritually or physically—and that you will send your Holy Spirit upon us to empower our prayers. Visibly demonstrate that your Church is on the side of life! Above all, let us, your children, know how much you love us.

And Mary, mother of Jesus, our "life, our sweetness and our hope," be with us now and always, bringing us health and joy in the midst of a world of sorrow. Be with us now and always and most especially at the hour of our death. Amen.

ADDENDUM

Many Catholics are probably not aware of a book published by the U.S. Bishop's Committee on the Liturgy entitled *Catholic Household Blessings and Prayers*.[17] This book is a collection of prayers—hundreds of them—that can be said by laypeople on the many ordinary occasions when there is an opportunity to pray together (such as "Parents' Thanksgiving for a Newborn Baby").

This book, then, supports our own work encouraging the laity to take a real role as leaders in praying for the sick. And this encouragement comes from the bishops themselves. As the editor, Bishop Donald Trautman, states in his introduction:

> The family is rightly called the "domestic church." It is in the family that we learn to recognize the love of God and learn to turn to him in prayer. . . . Families and other Catholic households should use this book as an aid to fulfill the Lord's command to pray always.

As you know, we have been encouraging you to be spontaneous and create your own heartfelt prayer when you pray for the sick, but some like to have a model for how they can pray. This book of Catholic prayers offers many prayers to use on various occasions. Bishop Trautman writes:

> This book is not intended to sit on a shelf unused. Every member of the household should know where to find it and should be encouraged to use it. Make it a part of family dinners and holiday celebrations, of bedtime routines and special occasions. Keep it in a central part of the house, along with the family Bible.

Here is one example of the type of prayer you will find—a prayer for an expectant mother. What a blessing it would be if husbands and wives would start praying for one another like this:

> God of love and compassion,
> look with favor on your daughter
> who anxiously awaits the birth of her child.
> Be with her in her labor
> that she may deliver her child safely
> and rest always in you.
> We ask this through Christ our Lord.
> Amen.[18]

ACKNOWLEDGMENTS

I want to thank all those who first told me about praying for the sick and how they had seen marvelous healings—both physical and emotional—when suffering people turned to Jesus in faith. Thank you especially to Jo Kimmel, Agnes Sanford and Tommy Tyson, who were among the first of those witnesses to God's love.

I would also like to thank those who joined with me on teams that traveled around the world to teach Catholics how to pray for healing. In 1964 Mrs. Barbara Shlemon Ryan became the first Catholic laywoman to become actively involved in praying for the sick. Sr. Jeanne Hill, OP, Sr. Mary Margaret McKenzie, and Fr. Michael Scanlan, TOR were also among the first Catholics to become involved. Catholics were especially receptive to this message because they had always believed in prayer to ask for God's help in meeting their human needs. The word quickly spread in a multitude of ways; for example, we formed the Association of Christian Therapists (ACT) to assist those in the healing professions, including physicians, nurses, psychiatrists and counselors, who want to pray to heal the sick. Several Catholics developed healing ministries and became widely known for their healing gifts, such as Sr. Briege McKenna, Fr. Ed McDonough, CSSR, and Fr. Ralph DiOrio.

Thirty-five thousand people attended the charismatic conference at Notre Dame in 1974, which focused on the theme of healing. Books on healing prayer appeared soon after, including Barbara Shlemon Ryan's *Healing Prayer* (republished by Servant Books in 2001) and the works of Jesuits Matt and Denny Linn. My first book on healing prayer, *Healing* (the 25th anniversary edition was published in 2009 by Ave Maria Press), came out in time for that conference. Conferences on healing soon touched the Church on every continent. I traveled to more than thirty countries with ecumenical healing teams.

This book on healing, written from a Catholic perspective, draws largely from my fifty years of experience and shared learning from friends in the healing ministry. At this point in time, my wife, Judith, and I are especially strengthened by the gifts of our staff at Christian Healing Ministries, known as CHM. We founded CHM in Clearwater, Florida, in 1983 and relocated to Jacksonville in 1987. Since then, the staff of CHM has grown to twenty, assisted by hundreds of trained prayer ministers. CHM offers schools that have trained thousands in the healing ministry, and alumni bring us new insights on prayer and also provide a loving community that gives us the strength and support we need to continue in this exciting ministry.

In particular, I want to thank Mrs. Gail Moseley of our CHM staff, who not only typed this book, but also made many helpful editorial comments.

My great hope in writing this book is that millions of Catholics around the world will be encouraged to pray to heal the sick, especially within their families.

Francis MacNutt, PhD
June 2010

Endnotes

1. I wrote a history of how the healing ministry was a major heritage of the early Church but how it gradually diminished: *The Healing Reawakening* (Grand Rapids, MI: Chosen Books, 2005).

2. Ramsey MacMullen, *Christianizing the Roman Empire,* A.D. 100–400 (New Haven, CT: Yale University Press, 1984), 27.

3. *Magnificat*, Volume 8, Number 14, March 2007, 214.

4. Bert Ghezzi, *Mystics and Miracles* (Chicago: Loyola Press, 2002), 108.

5. *Confronting the Devil's Power:* General Audience of Pope Paul VI, November 15, 1972. Accessed at www.ewtn.com/library/papaldoc/p6devil.htm.

6. Ramsey MacMullen, 60.

7. An entire 441–page history on this fascinating topic has been written: Marc Block, *The Royal Touch*, (New York: Dorset Press, 1989).

8. See Pope Benedict's *Regina Caeli* message, May 11, 2008, and his Message for World Youth Day 2008, issued on July 20, 2007, at www.vatican.va, as well as a report on his October 31, 2008 meeting with those attending a conference on the Catholic Charismatic Renewal, reported by Zenit at http://zenit.org/article-24123?l=english.

9. Spiritualism is turning to a spiritual source other than God for spiritual assistance, such as holding a séance to discover, through the help of a medium, the spiritual state of someone who is dead.

10. Chester Tolson, Ph.D., and Harold Koenig, M.D., *The Healing Power of Prayer* (Grand Rapids, MI: Baker Books, 2003), 28.

11. "Effects of Intercessory Prayer on Patients with Rheumatoid Arthritis," Dale A. Matthews, MD, Sally M. Marlowe, NP, and Francis S. MacNutt, Ph.D. *Southern Medical Journal*, Volume 93, Number 12, December 2000, 1177–1186.

12. For anyone who would like to see how we prayed with the patients and how some of them improved, you can order the DVD *Shall We Pray?* from the bookstore of Christian Healing Ministries at (904) 765–3332.

13. Larry Dossey, M.D., *Prayer is Good Medicine* (New York: HarperCollins, 1996), 66.

14. "Anointing of the Sick," *The Encyclopedia of Catholicism*, Richard P. McBrien, general editor (New York: HarperCollins, 1995), 57–61.

15. Agnes Sanford, *The Healing Light*, revised edition (St. Paul, MN: MacAlester Park Publishing Co., 1972), 89.

16. Martos, Joseph. *Doors to the Sacred: A Historical Introduction to Sacraments in the Catholic Church*. Liguori, MO: Liguori/Triumph, 2001), 331.

17. Bishop Donald Trautman, editor, *Catholic Household Blessings and Prayers*, revised edition (U.S. Conference on the Liturgy, Washington, D.C., 2008).

18. Ibid., 234.

ABOUT CHRISTIAN HEALING MINISTRIES

Christian Healing Ministries, founded by Francis and Judith MacNutt, seeks to advance our Lord's ministry of healing through prayer. CHM, which is located in Jacksonville, Florida, is dedicated to praying with those in need of healing in the physical, emotional, and spiritual areas of their lives and to teaching others about this often overlooked aspect of Christ's ministry.

For more information, go to
www.christianhealingministries.org.

Francis' books are also available at this Web site.

theWORD
among us®
The *Spirit* of Catholic Living

This book was published by The Word Among Us. Since 1981, The Word Among Us has been answering the call of the Second Vatican Council to help Catholic laypeople encounter Christ in the Scriptures.

The name of our company comes from the prologue to the Gospel of John and reflects the vision and purpose of all of our publications: to be an instrument of the Spirit, whose desire is to manifest Jesus' presence in and to the children of God. In this way, we hope to contribute to the Church's ongoing mission of proclaiming the gospel to the world so that all people would know the love and mercy of our Lord and grow ever more deeply in love with him.

Our monthly devotional magazine, *The Word Among Us*, features meditations on the daily and Sunday Mass readings, and currently reaches more than one million Catholics in North America and another half million Catholics in one hundred countries around the world. Our book division, The Word Among Us Press, publishes numerous books, Bible studies, and pamphlets that help Catholics grow in their faith.

To learn more about who we are and what we publish, log on to our website at www.wau.org. There you will find a variety of Catholic resources that will help you grow in your faith.

Embrace His Word, Listen to God . . .